Red

Red | **Architecture in Monochrome**

Φ

Seeing Red, Everywhere

Stella Paul

Red is fundamental to who we are. It flows through our veins as blood, coloring the insides of our bodies and circulating through our interior thoughts. It can flush skin to reveal emotions, from anger to embarrassment to desire. Blood's red, a life force, signals the color's power and vitality. But whichever visceral first impressions we have, there are layers of further nuance, questions, and surprises. Even elemental blood—this intimate way into the topic—has additional story lines. Not all animals even have red blood. Some marine creatures have blue–colored blood; some worms bleed green, others violet. But the human condition is red.

The hue has remarkable variety, even when considered apart from any personal or cultural references. Color is simply a measurable manifestation of light—of how we interpret wavelengths of electromagnetic energy. The red our human eyes see is at one edge of the color spectrum, comprising wavelengths of about 625 to 740 nanometers. In that little swathe, though, lies enormous breadth of expression, and distinctions we hardly have words for, let alone shared, universal impressions. Red encompasses everything from terracotta, russet, burgundy, oxblood to puce, and ranges also from scarlet to vermilion, crimson to carmine. It can be darker or paler, drabber or brighter, densely saturated or diaphanously translucent. That describes a mere smattering of red's many characteristics. A given red might be tinged toward orange or blue, or interact with neighboring colors to effect staggering turnabout. Red can be subtle or caustic; it can whisper or shriek. In any case, it's a polyphony, not a monotone. As artist Josef Albers wrote, if fifty people were to hear the word "red," fifty reds would come to mind: "And one can be sure that all these reds will be very different."

Red is significant wherever we look. In art, varieties of red color were humans' earliest creations and continue to fuel the most modern expression. Thinking about how and why a color is generated as a material substance and how it's used in art or technology leads to social and intellectual arenas in which red plays starring roles. Whether the semi–secretive technical processes and philosophies of alchemists' studios, where red was instrumental in a process of metamorphosis, or dyers' workshops, where civic regulations charted how red was made and who used it, the by-products of red drove economies and behavior. Red has also occupied an important place in spiritual and religious practice from antiquity to the present. Within those forums, red is as multivalent as the diverse shades of its hue, reflecting attitudes about sin and redemption, lust and romance, charity and benevolence, fervor and play, courage and sacrifice, murder and damnation. Equally, red holds sway through customs and idioms, in everyday comportment whether elite or abject, in politics and revolution, and in formulating national identity. Red is embedded in literature and fairy tale, and it has also served in promoting consumerism and public safety. It lies at the edge of the color spectrum, but red is central in much thought and action. It's been described by Renaissance naturalists as "the color of colors" and in modern times as "primary." Red warrants a closer look.

"India contributes the ooze of her rivers and the blood of dragons and elephants."
Pliny the Elder, AD 23–79

What does red come from? And where? Material choices that artists make about pigments are meaningful. Understanding origins opens up ideas about value, technology, and philosophy. One form of red has always been among the planet's most ubiquitous substances: soft rock deposits of silica, clay, and iron oxides. Other varieties have been rare and costly, exacting significant human toll, produced with secrecies and mysticisms.

Working with red is a primeval impulse. Using the red of iron oxides (dense hematite coloring softer ochre) Paleolithic artists conjured an inscrutable art of undeniable beauty on walls and ceilings in caves tens of thousands of years ago. These prehistoric artists were technologists, presiding over a multitiered process to invent the material for their art—first identifying iron-rich deposits, then extracting the raw goods from the earth, grinding it to powder, even heating it to alter coloration, and then inventing the means to make powder into paint that adheres to surfaces. No material comes ready-made, not even pervasive ochre: present at our species' threshold. Making red

shows brilliant mastery. Red ochre continues to be a widely used substance; in some cultures it carries deep spiritual resonance. Sacred ochre deposits in Australia are vital to ancestral cosmologies, and access to these sites and the colors they produce is strictly controlled. Beautiful aboriginal art tells stories of heritage and belief, with red color a key subject.

Wealthy ancient Romans sought out the rarest reds to decorate opulent villas in Pompeii. The more exuberant the color, the better. Naturalist Pliny the Elder railed against florid tastes and exotic, excessively expensive sourcing. Romans had several duller reds readily at hand, but artists and patrons wanted a special red derived from cinnabar. They had to get this luxury from Spain, where this highly toxic principal ore of mercury was mined, draining health and wealth.

Pliny's reference to "dragon's blood" is both polemic and legend. Mythic stories about where red comes from persist across time and culture. Accounts about comingling blood from dragons and elephants to create a resinous red extend from antiquity through the Middle Ages in Europe. A color by that name, made from plants, is still available.

Medieval artists embraced vermilion, a dazzling orangey-red which is a product of alchemy. Alchemists were proto-chemists whose work in extracting and transforming materials was coupled with metaphorical, symbolic thought—and hermetic language. With an ultimate goal of turning base metal into gold, alchemists engaged in "operations," each with stages of color change. Red plays a role in one of the final stages; one alchemist wrote about seeking the "red elixir." Along the way pigments were synthesized. Sulfur and mercury, two of alchemy's essential building blocks, could be heated precisely to bond together into a new union: vermilion.

"[Scarlet is] the first and the highest and the most important color that we have."
Fifteenth-century Florentine dyers' manual

"Scarlet" didn't always denote a specific hue. It originally designated a luxury cloth: not exclusively red. The gorgeous textile and its most alluring color option became synonymous, and eventually the word attached to the color itself. It was fabric worn by societies' upper strata. Europe's medieval kings and princes wore red. Sumptuous red mantles and other garments figured in coronations in England, Scotland, Poland, and Sicily. It accrued to other designated groups of individuals, too, as signal of rank or authority—with some twists over the course of centuries, especially when religion and law attempted to codify behaviors.

Creating intensely saturated, colorfast red cloth is no small matter. Finding the colorant is the first crucial step, and as with pigments, sourcing has major implications. The pinnacle for red cloth originates with tiny parasites. Europe's special red, kermes, is made by crushing dried bodies of female insects living in types of oaks around Eastern Europe and the Mediterranean. There are biblical references to cloth of this derivation. Roman generals wore scarlet cloaks: the privilege of rank. Later, vassals made feudal payments in it to medieval lords. Cloth production was licensed and regulated according to color and type of fabric. Guilds for medieval dyers strictly separated those who worked in red from their counterparts who worked in blue.

A similar red, cochineal, has deep history in Central and South America, where other insects infest prickly-pear cacti. Under the Incas, rulers alone wore special cochineal garments and headpieces, and received substantial quantities of it as tribute from subjects. Cochineal's attractions brought two cultures together—consequentially. With the arrival of Spanish conquistadors in the sixteenth century, New World luxury goods enticed Old World tastes. Spain monopolized a huge global trade in a red commodity that proved irresistible from Europe to the Middle East. Cochineal propelled an empire. In 1587 alone, 72 metric tonnes of it came through Seville.

Whether kermes or cochineal, red clothed elites. But red also became a color related to saints and sinners, and a color intensively regulated. By 1245 Pope Innocent IV gave cardinals their red hats; dressing in red from head to toe was decreed in 1464. The Catholic Church had designated it the color of martyrdom, to evoke spilled blood and the sacrifice it represents. Mary Queen of Scots sent the same message at her execution in 1587, revealing her crimson red bodice and petticoat. Color wars permeated the Protestant Reformation. Sober black eclipsed tastes for red, and churches were "cleansed" of color. Red became associated with the theater of Catholic rites. Luther decried the Pope as "the red whore of Babylon," referencing The Bible's Book of Revelation and a passage describing a woman dressed in scarlet sitting on a scarlet beast. Red also equates to hellfire and many vices, including at least four of the seven deadly sins: pride, lust, anger, and gluttony.

In everyday matters, red had long been a presence at both ends of the behavioral or economic spectrum. Sumptuary laws further elaborated the matter. Codes regulated who could wear which colors or textiles, demarcating class and status, controlling ruinous expenditures for luxury products, and signaling message. In a time when princes wore glorious red, others—some classified as marginal or even outcast—wore bits of red identifiers. Butchers might have a red insignia; prostitutes might wear a red scarf. Centuries later, Hawthorne's *The Scarlet Letter* still marked sexual infraction. Even today, we refer to a city's "red light district."

Wearing red cloth or ornamentation has denoted rank, spiritual meaning, power, and authority even as it just as authoritatively connects to vice or indiscretion.

"O my Luve's like a red, red rose."
Robert Burns, *A Red, Red Rose*, 1794

As central motif or eloquent metaphor, red in literature embraces the color's many through-lines, from gentle to violent.

With the finding of a red rose in an enclosed garden, a challenging search for love is finally realized in one of the most enduringly popular poems in medieval Europe. The allegorical *Roman de la Rose*, written in thirteenth–century France, is an exposition of courtly love with red at its culmination. The literary trope connecting red roses with ideas about love is perennial. Five centuries later, Robert Burns published *A Red, Red Rose*, with its famous opening line and compellingly tangible description of the ineffable: what it feels like to fall in love. Burns, a tenant farmer and poet–songwriter, drew inspiration from Scottish folklore and country song, and was devoted to the preservation of tradition even as he appropriated it. Burns's tender red rose is steadfast metaphor, even today.

Red is not always sweet. Shakespeare invented a new word-form around it for Macbeth, who speculates that his bloodstained hands would "the multitudinous seas incarnadine, making the green one red." With a new verb generated from an existing adjective describing pinkish-crimson, a vast green sea would "incarnadine" rather than wash away murder's bloody residue.

Like the metaphor of the red rose, blood's redness is endlessly charismatic. In Edgar Allen Poe's 1842 *Masque of the Red Death*, the horror is conveyed through color symbolism in rooms of various hues, and crescendos with death (for all), which comes to the party in a shroud-like costume, graphically "besprinkled with scarlet blood." Poe's "Red Death" is fictitious plague, colored in red's high pitch; historical plague is "black."

Red is central to fairy tales, too. Little Red Riding Hood's red cloak isn't merely a fashion statement. It suggests symbolic meaning. Is it redolent of dangers, bloody violence, or other unseemly acts that the bad wolf will commit against grandmother and child?

Red marks the occasion at many of life's important junctures. It also inserts itself into our daily habits and idioms, coloring everyday language.

"Any red is rooted in blood, glass, wine, hunters' caps, and a thousand other concrete phenomena."
Robert Motherwell, 1915–1991

Evidence of burial customs shows red playing a role far back in time. The red substances that prehistoric artists used to make cave paintings have also been found in burial pits that might have been dug a hundred thousand years ago. In ancient Egyptian tombs, we find red linen wrappings as well as white. Virgil's *Aeneid*, the epic poem celebrating deep ancestries and cultural foundation, describes ancient funeral practices that included depositing red-colored things. At his father's tomb, Aeneas pours two bowls of red wine and "two more of hallowed blood, then scatters crimson flowers." In the Americas, the Maya placed red cinnabar objects and powder in tombs.

But it's not only a color to punctuate the end of life. Red is often a vivid marker to celebrate the robust or the promising. Brides in China and South Asia traditionally wear red. In ancient Rome they wore flame-colored veils. In many cultures red garments are worn at the most festive occasions and red accoutrements decorate bodies and spaces. From long before Cleopatra, to the men and women of the court of Versailles, to Marilyn Monroe, people have "rouged" lips and cheeks; victorious Roman generals colored their faces red; Santa Claus's red suit stands for jolly Christmas holidays. Celebrated individuals are welcomed with a red carpet; to "paint the town red" is to indulge in especially flamboyant extravagance. Red can augur prosperity: red envelopes hold gifts of money in China, where red is joyous. It can also symbolize cherished values, color–coded into the narrative in paintings from Lorenzetti to Rubens depicting specific biblical or mythical stories.

Red plays negative, too. We see "see red" when feeling angry, we get "red-faced" when we get embarrassed, and sometimes get caught "red-handed" in misdeeds. We bemoan the frustrating "red-tape" of bureaucracy. Bullfighters wave red capes to taunt bulls (who happen to be colorblind to red).

"Beat the Whites with the Red Wedge."
Bolshevik poster designed by El Lissitzky, 1919

Color can be a call to mobilize. By the 1790s, red's association with aristocracy had diminished and it was identified with fervent social changes. French revolutionaries donned red caps styled after those they thought were worn by freed Roman slaves. They arrogated the red flag that government had used to dictate disbursement during siege ("the bloody flag of tyranny"). Red flags had been used since the Middle Ages to signal "no surrender" or "no mercy." Now they were emblems of change. By the mid-nineteenth century, red was adopted by socialists throughout Europe, and by 1917 red was the color of the Russian Revolution. Russia made its national flag red; red became the color of the Communist Party in China, Vietnam, and elsewhere. But communism has no lock on red. Red is so compelling as a color for expressing national identity that it's a major component on 70 percent of the United Nations current members' flags—from Norway to Samoa to Tunisia.

Red commands public action in other, ubiquitous, ways. Municipal authorities use it in signage to ensure public safety. We take notice when we see conspicuous red. Red stop signs, worldwide, convey orders, aiming to control behavior and reduce road accidents. Astrophysicist Neil deGrasse Tyson suggests deep roots: "If our blood used copper instead of iron, turning it green, I wonder what color we would have made stop lights and stop signs." Red traffic signs tell us what to do; the insistent red used prevalently in marketing tries to tell us what to buy, urging us to connect with product. Perhaps it's red's perfectly understood exuberance and its intimate link with our lifeblood that make the color perform so well in branding and advertising.

Red convokes. Its siren voice can stir revolution, it can caution and protect, and it can loosen purse strings—all at once.

"A power-house in the shape of a red brick chair 90 feet high."
William Carlos Williams, *Classic Scene*, 1937

There's a pop of red everywhere. From temple to fort, rustic cottage to industrial powerhouse, urban high-rise to country barn, red is abundant today and in the historical record. Using red to construct shelter reaches further back, to the millennia before recorded histories. Why red? Early builders used the products of the earth that were also seminal in making art: oxides in clays. Just as with art or cloth, thinking about red's material substance and sourcing is a gateway for insights about buildings. In fact, red has served builders and architects through all the perspectives suggested in this introduction, as a protean voice in expressing message and meaning, metaphor and technology, identity and cultural tastes.

Actually, red needn't "pop." It can be understated: of the earth and blending right in. For millennia, clay rich in iron oxide has been formed into reddish, sunbaked mud bricks. Heated in kilns, bricks' redness intensifies. Romans' extensive brick production created a product that colored a great swathe of antiquity, and red brick has never lost its utility or allure as building material. From brick Gothic in the Baltics and Scandinavia to New York's Puck Building or Moscow's State Historical Museum in the nineteenth century, to houses,

complexes, and public facilities built today, the earliest human-made building material shapes red-earth structures everywhere.

Sweden's signature red on barns, cottages, and also a celebrated church stems from the ingenious transformation of byproducts of regional mining. Mounds of iron-based cinder refuse were reborn as red paint when mixed with oil, flour, and water. Not only resourceful and aesthetically pleasing, this red functions as protection against rot and infestation. Vernacular red barns punctuate the American landscape too, where a different paint recipe was contrived in the late 1700s. Many other red concoctions have been invented with taste and function in mind. And red traditions have been creatively appropriated and reinvented. This book includes stunning examples: from little red cottages in entirely unexpected new contexts such as a clapboard house perched on top of a tower in Suffolk, England, to several barn-like structures reconceived as elegant contemporary homes or complexes in urban or rural settings, or O'Gorman's masterful application of Mexican folkloric color made integral to Modernist esthetics.

Various red building materials become intrinsic to places or epochs, coloring their histories and inflecting new approaches. Plasters, paints, sandstones, or bricks tint neighborhoods and even cities in reddish tonality, which provides inspiration and counterpoint for new building. Jaipur's tint is pink and red sandstone, and also calcium oxide compound. New buildings can echo natural contexts, as examples in Portugal, Cologne, and elsewhere show, taking the colors of local soil as base-color for other materials. The tonality of sand dunes and walled desert environments in North Africa is muse to fascinating reapplications in milieus worldwide. New red materials, constantly generated, offer new palettes—from blazingly bright to discreetly nuanced. Technologies like pre-rusted steel, powder-coated zinc, pigmented concrete, lacquers, glittery resins, LED lights, new polymers, or even compressed paper carry color through whole neighborhoods, or stand in striking juxtaposition to their contexts.

Many buildings in this book communicate red's metaphorical messaging, honoring cultural identity and evoking fanciful links. The red monument in Qingdao's May Fourth Square is graphic testament to cultural and political ideologies. A pavilion with serpentine form and tiled, scale-like cladding celebrates China's associations with dragons; a theater shaped like a giant lantern renders cultural heritage as form. A flaming red hotel in Eindhoven plays on its proximity to the city's red-light district; the whimsy of *Touch of Evil*, a jarringly red tunnel under a highway, erases danger and discomfort. Shades of red wine varietals tint buildings associated with winemaking, and three shades of blood are represented in tones of ceramic tile at a collection center in Poland. The plush interior of a rock museum suggests a guitar case's velvet lining; a large space carpeted in red brings new scale and permanence to the welcome of a red carpet.

A fire station in Puerto Rico and a fire-services center in Cologne draw on red's long-standing associations with heat and urgency—and with fiery red's authority in civic signage in warning and commanding attention. Equally, summoning attention is integral in commerce and business. A screeching-red shopping mall in Russia, shaped like a barcode, reinforces its message; corporate branding goes full-scale to the size of buildings with facilities for Nestlé and pavilions for Coca-Cola and Miele.

Some buildings are intended to play on the color's formal attributes—whether in investigating red's effect in a green landscape as the interaction of two complementary colors or in exploiting an intensely saturated red's capacity to obliterate detail and flatten volume. Many celebrate the fact that red can be disruptive—in dynamically positive ways. Apposing surrounding environments, bright red is a spotlight, whether to a private house on an otherwise neutral Italian city street, the unexpected note of a red bridge in an English landscape, a carefully dispersed series of focal points throughout a large Paris complex, or a vibrant neuropsychiatric clinic beckoning in Spain. This color's extroversion elicits action, a reminder that we move through and around the built environment. Red pathways guide passage, leading people through numerous gardens, across bridges, and even into spirituality, as with vermilion torii gates straddling a network of trails at a Shinto shrine or a pulsating red sanctuary in a Buddhist temple. Exploiting the color's dynamism, several theaters and creative activity centers are boldly, exuberantly red inside and out. Some of these structures are mobile or temporary; perhaps impermanence gives all the more license to red's proclivity to grab attention.

Even a glimpse at red's history—in architecture, art, ideology, or thought—shows one thing: the color has an uncanny facility to speak clearly, but communicate widely divergent stories. Sometimes it can even say two things at once. In Russian, for example, "red" and "beautiful" share a common root, which is a fitting conflation for the contents of this book about red architecture.

"Red protects itself. No color is as territorial. It stakes a claim, is on the alert against the spectrum."

Derek Jarman | **Film Director, Artist, and Author (1942–1994)**

Casa das Artes | **Future Architecture Thinking**
Miranda do Corvo, Portugal
2013

Cultural buildings can shout, though most choose not to. The Casa das Artes, in the inland Portuguese town of Miranda do Corvo, bucks this trend: it's angular, dynamic, and rendered bright crimson outside, as well as partly inside. Its dramatic, sloping roofline echoes the distant mountain, Lousã, and the shape of nearby rooftops. In the context of its site, it stands as a symbol; a meeting place for people. The Casa das Artes is more than a building, a shelter, or a place to exhibit art; it's a landmark for, and a celebration of, community—people, after all, meet in built environments. Stimulative of creative thought and action, the building's bright-red, performative character is a call to action—surrounded by roads and a sloping parkland, it's a curiosity. In the homogeneous shade of its surface, it stands apart from its neighbors as a place that represents each citizen's creativity.

Bressuire Theater | **Archidev**
| **Bressuire, France**
| **2012**

This 350-seat theater was opened in Bressuire, western France, in a slightly elevated position on the site of a former livestock market. The theater consists of a low, box-like podium with glazed facade for the entrance foyer, on top of which sits a large drum structure holding the auditorium and part of the stage tower. 14,531 square feet (1,350 square meters) in area, it includes rehearsal and exhibition spaces, performers' dressing rooms, and arts-administration offices. The bright red of the exterior continues to the interior, with large swathes of the color in the foyer, flowing through to the auditorium's vibrantly upholstered red seats, with the rest of the space being clad in beautifully austere pale wood. The theater is the center of a regional initiative, Scènes de Territoire, which supports the arts scene in the area known as the Bocage Bressuirais. It stages dance, drama, circus arts, comedy, and other performances. Archidev, the practice behind the design, specializes in innovative cultural projects. The theater's bold red color was controversial; several months after opening, the local council received notice from the French association of architects, ANABF, that the theater was "out of character with its environment" and requesting immediate remedy. However, the theater today remains gloriously, defiantly red.

Nuestra Señora del Carmen Neuropsychiatric Center | **José Javier Gallardo**
Zaragoza, Spain
2011

This striking clinic for young people with psychiatric disorders was built as an extension to Nuestra Señora del Carmen Neuropsychiatric Center in Zaragoza, Spain. Designed by José Javier Gallardo of g.bang architects (whose maxim is "in search of sexy architecture"), the building houses accommodation and social spaces for patients, along with staff quarters. A long, low building, its spiked pitched roofs form a jagged, quirky profile against the cerulean Spanish sky. The different roof-forms demarcate the zones and areas of activity below them. The highest-pitched roofs are above the common room; the less steeply angled gables above the bedrooms; and the flat roofs are above the staff quarters. The facility will eventually be extended to include workshops. The building makes a bold statement that flies in the face of stereotypical perceptions of clinics for those suffering from mental illness; it's striking, highly conspicuous, and unique. The carmine zinc-coated exterior shouts about its existence and is meant, according to the architects, to make the center's guests visible: it "robs us of prejudice" and "emphasizes the social work" that goes on there. This greater visibility and acceptance of their condition will ultimately help the patients' healing, they say.

Barcode | **Vitruvius and Sons**
St. Petersburg, Russia
2007

The barcode was invented by Bernard Silver in 1948 and is now a ubiquitous part of modern life. Highly symbolic of consumer culture, it has been used in works by American artist Scott Blake and English graffiti artist Banksy, but it's also a form that has inspired architects. Vitruvius and Sons have designed this bright-red shopping mall in St. Petersburg, Russia, adopting the barcode as an apt motif for the store, a vibrant beacon surrounded by otherwise uniform, gray, concrete structures. Barcode is located on Narodnaya Ulitsa, in the middle of a Soviet residential area near the Lomonosov Metro. 59,200 square feet (5,500 square meters) in area, built in 2007, the mall has four floors of shops, with a further two floors above. The cut-out numbers on the facade at the sixth floor are actual windows; the numeric code that forms the design doesn't have any deeper significance or meaning when scanned; however, this does not detract from the considerable visual impact. The barcode motif has been used on several other buildings' designs worldwide—hardly surprising given the massive impact digitization has had on the world.

Parc de la Villette | **Bernard Tschumi**
Paris, France
1987

Once the 125-acre (50-hectare) site of the French national wholesale meat-market, later abandoned, the home of the now world-renowned Parc de la Villette in Paris was poised for new development in the early 1980s. Its architect, who fought off fierce international competition for the commission, envisioned the landscape as a place in which natural and artificial elements—such as buildings and infrastructure—could intelligently merge while, at the same time, existing in tension in a persistent state of emerging reconfiguration. The architect designed over twenty five buildings and follies for the park, which were often described as a collective. In this way, Parc de la Villette should be considered a single, discontinuous, building—a constellation of connected spaces in which its functions overlap. Museums, outdoor movie theaters, playgrounds, and parkland converge to create a spectacular assemblage of points of interest in which the "red line" is the color red itself. The architects' choosing of the color leads from the need to define the park as separate from, but connected to, Paris; a place contrasted to but continued from, in one way or another, the language of the city's distinct urban form. In another way, red represents the color of revolution: this project, in scale and in scope, contributed to a global reframing of the meaning of parkland and public space.

The Shed | **Haworth Tompkins**
London, England, UK
2013

The Shed, a temporary addition to London's iconic National Theatre, was designed to push creative boundaries both as a building and in what occupied its spaces. Described by its architects as "a testbed for experiment," the project embodied lofty ambitions and intelligent spatial design. A truncated cube ascended in the form of four towers, all clad in bright, uniform, crimson wood. Designed to refer to the facade of the adjacent National Theatre building proper, which was cast out of board-marked concrete to emulate the texture and grain of wood, The Shed stood as a highly visible beacon on the city's South Bank. For the architects, the project resembled more of a performance than a usual design challenge. Inside, a 225-seat auditorium built from raw steel and plywood belied the spectacle of the structure itself. No doors or windows were visible to passersby; finding the entrance was a puzzle. It represented a uniquely bold gesture, almost entirely sustainably produced and, as a result, reusable. The Shed represents the principle that even when in dialogue with a venerable, much-loved building (the National Theatre), a structure can still make a statement and, in so doing, elevate its surroundings.

The Opéra Garnier Restaurant | **Odile Decq**
Paris, France
2011

Palais Garnier was designed to be the Paris Opera House by Charles Garnier. As part of his plan, he proposed creating a restaurant in the Rotonde du Glacier, a cool and luminous Belle Epoque space tucked behind the colonnades of the opera's east facade. For budgetary reasons, it never happened. In the twentieth century, two more attempts to build a restaurant, in 1973 and 1992, failed. Odile Decq, responding to a commission in 2008, had a challenging brief in such a highly sensitive setting. In response, she created a two-floor, dramatic, freestanding fiberglass structure surrounded by a glass facade. It forms a new, curving mezzanine level, supported by tree-like pillars. The encircling glass veil appears to float unsupported, but is

connected, via a single strip of bent steel, to supporting rods driven into the cornices of the rotunda's pillars. The architect likened its blob-like white forms to an "insidious phantom"—one that has silently crept and expanded into the space. Soft furnishings are a stunning opera red, which works in opposition to the dazzling white structure. The restaurant's futuristic, organic forms create an effective tension with the rotunda's Napoleon III-style architecture; the entire installation is completely removable if necessary. Odile Decq won the 2016 Jane Drew Prize for women architects and was hailed a "creative powerhouse, spirited breaker of rules, and advocate of equality."

Museum MUMAC | **Arkispazio**
Milan, Italy
2012

Coffee has a unique place in Italian culture, and MUMAC is a museum that celebrates the development and history of the coffee machine. It was built to mark the centenary of one of Italy's largest coffee-machine manufacturers, Cimbali. The company was established by Giuseppe Cimbali in 1912 in Milan; the earliest coffee makers were "column machines" with coal- or wood-fired vertical boilers. Since those early days, Cimbali has grown into a huge business with three factories producing 200 machines a day. MUMAC is located in the grounds of Cimbali's headquarters and production plant near Milan, occupying a former warehouse, which was specially converted into a visitor attraction. The museum space is a rectangular block that has been given a sinuous new shell supported on a lattice frame; the visitor enters via a curving, high-walled corridor leading up to the main entrance. There is an exhibition space, a library known as "world of coffee," with an archive of 15,000 documents related to the subject, and a museum with 200 coffee machines, occupying in total 19,375 square feet (1,800 square meters). The facade is clad in composite metal strips in the brand color of Cimbali—scarlet—which are arranged to suggest the flowing movement of poured coffee. The purpose of the space means there is no need for major openings in the facade—as a result, there are simply horizontal slits between the metal panels. At night, they create a backlit grid of light.

Y House | **Steven Holl**
| **Catskill, New York State, USA**
| **1999**

Views of endless countryside unfurl beyond this weekend retreat in a remote part of the Catskill Mountains, New York State. The Y-shaped home is, says architect Steven Holl, "like a found stick making a primitive mark on the landscape." Holl has integrated various references to rural architecture into the home's design. Viewed from the side, with its sloping roof and small openings, it looks like a barn—an effect reinforced by the stained cedar paneling on the sides of the house, and its iron-oxide steel framing and roof. This is a direct reference to the lead-red color used on barn buildings in the area, but also gives the home a a certain warmth and vibrancy. The two deep, open balconies face almost due south; high canopies on both shade the living areas from the hot summer sun, while the open balcony sides allow the lower winter sun to penetrate deep into the house, to amplify the heat coming from it. A priority for the clients was to surround themselves with art, and the Y-shape allows more wall space for hanging a contemporary collection. The two adjoining wings create a sense of togetherness while maintaining some separation—ideal if a group is using the house for the weekend. The space doesn't feel box-like or constraining, but branches out in an organic way, like a tree. Ash lines the ceilings and floors to create a brilliantly light, natural-feeling space.

Parque de Bombas | Lt. Col. Maximo Meana
Ponce, Puerto Rico
1882

Ponce, in southern Puerto Rico, is, after the capital San Juan, the island's most populous metropolitan area. In 1820, two fires broke out in the city: one in the center, the other in the port, bringing trade to a virtual standstill. In response, in 1863, the governor of Ponce, Don Miguel de la Torre, ordered that every male in the town between the ages of 16 and 60 spent compulsory unpaid time serving in a new fire brigade. In 1882, an important trade exhibition was held in Ponce and the Parque de Bombas was constructed as the main pavilion, designed by Spanish solider Maximo Meana, also a trained architect, and later mayor of Ponce, reflecting the esteem in which the town's fire service was held. In 1885, the pavilion was repurposed as the town's main fire station. Facing the Plaza Las Delicias, the building is rectangular in form, with two towers at the front and narrow, slit-like openings giving it a Moorish look. Victorian influences can be seen in the ornate decorative moldings on the roof overhang and fanlight windows. Clad in wood painted red and black, the city's colors, it has a curiously whimsical appearance, more fun-house than firehouse. In 1990, the fire service relocated, and after a restoration led by architect Paul O'Neill Ojeda, the building was reopened as a museum. It's now an important cultural center for the city.

Vibeeng School | **Arkitema Architects**
Haslev, Denmark
2014

Haslev, a small town in south Zealand, takes education seriously: despite having only around 11,000 inhabitants, the locality boasts eleven schools. Vibeeng, a combined infant and primary school for 500 pupils, is a recent, impressive, addition. Designed by Arkitema Architects with a focus on integrating pedagogy and sustainability, the complex is in the shape of an irregular star. The school's roofs are angled at varying pitches in such a way as to allow solar panels on the south-facing sides and light wells to face north—a plan to ensure low energy consumption. These irregular roof spaces also provide a dynamic space inside the school. The facade is clad with panels in three different shades of red, creating a quirky and ever-changing striped pattern across the building. The exterior space is geared towards play and socializing, with decked areas for hanging out, and landscaped, grassy, and wooded areas for running around. Inside, the bright colors continue with the use of acidic and sunshine yellows, blues, and yet more red on the walls. The main entrance takes you straight into a double-height, multipurpose central atrium, a warmly social space known as the "heart room." Its focus is on gatherings and events for the school and its community; all of the building's different areas flow from this.

HVC KringloopEnergie Recycling Center | **Groosman**
Dordrecht, The Netherlands
2012

This project was part renovation, part new-build for HVC KringloopEnergie, a Dutch sustainable-energy company, and the largest non-commercial waste collector in the Netherlands. HVC generate renewable energy—heat, electricity, and gas—from waste, biomass, wind, solar, and geothermal sources. This recycling depot sorts through all kinds of deliveries from the local areas—electronic equipment, plastics, paper, and food waste. This bright-red building is the reception to the plant, and also houses offices. Its vibrant exterior makes it unmissable in a monotonous industrial landscape and establishes an obvious arrival point for vehicles, thus keeping the plant's workflow efficient. Trucks check in here and are then directed to the appropriate part of the facility. A series of four barn-like warehouses are positioned at right angles to the reception, and clad in austere, black, corrugated steel, forming a strong visual contrast in terms both of volume and color. Here, rubbish is unloaded, sorted into containers, and taken away for further processing. Appropriately for a recycling depot, IFD (Industrial, Flexible, and Detachable) construction has been used throughout, which means the buildings' components are easy to dismantle and can be reused in future.

Music Royale | **Peter Johansson**
| **Liverpool, England, UK**
| **2004**

Garish, twee, and apparently popular with local cab drivers, this pavilion, designed by Swedish artist Peter Johansson for the 2004 Liverpool Biennial of Contemporary Art, became a symbol of the festival. An archetypal Swedish summer house, this prefabricated wooden hut, transplanted to the South Lawn near to the Pier Head in Liverpool, was painted in a shouting tone Johansson calls "Swedish Red" (falu red, the famous paint used on Swedish wooden buildings, is much more muted). Loud in another way, ABBA's "Dancing Queen" was pumped from the cabin's loudspeakers day and night. The pavilion had a kitchen and bathroom, but was otherwise unfurnished to allow the curious to gather inside. According to the artist, it was meant to attract visitors "like bait", and was an ironic comment on the mass-produced pop and flatpack consumer culture of his native Sweden. Dwarfed next to Walter Aubrey Thomas's Royal Liver Building, Music Royale was a bold affront to the 1911 building's stony gray. Everything in the pavilion's interior—walls, floor, stove, refrigerator, bath, and even toilet—was also painted in a lurid red. Some saw this as a reference to Liverpool's far-left government of the 1970s; others to Liverpool Football Club's colors. Fans of Everton F.C. (the rival team also based in the city), took exception to its not being blue. The biennial was hailed as a success, and instrumental in the city being named 2008 European Capital of Culture.

Terra | **Orly Genger**
Oklahoma City, Oklahoma, USA
2014

This sinuous installation was on display in Oklahoma City between 2014 and 2016. With Terra, Orly Genger was inspired by the vast scale and red earth of Oklahoma's landscape. Genger is known for her spectacular public artworks using recycled lobster-fishing rope, which she knits, weaves, and molds into gigantic site–specific pieces. In Terra, she used a staggering 265 miles (427 kilometers) of rope and 350 gallons (1,600 liters) of terracotta-colored paint to depict the "red dirt" of Oklahoma, suggesting, she said, "the clay-like nature of the earth, and ... the bricks with which we build walls." Thus notions of the natural and man-made fuse in one piece, underscored by the synthetic fibers lying in close contact with grass and tree bark. The sculpture worked on different scales: it was gargantuan in Campbell Park, just north of Oklahoma City's downtown; visitors could loop in and out of its curves and feel overpowered in its otherness; and perhaps, in a play on words, it created a sense of terror. But close up, it resembled chain mail or knitted wool, indicating the staggering hours of human toil behind it. As time passed, the wonder evoked by Terra shifted to pathos: it faded, weathered, and slumped, and its skeleton (steel stakes and zip ties) became visible.

"When I haven't any blue, I use red."

Pablo Picasso | **Artist (1881–1973)**

"When I haven't any blue, I use red."

Nestlé Chocolate Museum | **Rojkind Arquitectos**
Toluca de Lerdo, Mexico
2007

Nestlé invited Michel Rojkind to design an external corridor to funnel the flow of visitors—mostly very excited children—to the chocolate-production lines at its factory near Toluca de Lerdo. Rather than creating a purely functional solution, Rojkind had the idea of making the walkway into an entire visitor experience, complete with auditorium, exhibits, and a gift shop—all packaged in a way that would appeal to children. The result was a 984-feet (300-meter) elevated walkway, twisting and turning toward the delights of the chocolate factory. Resting on splayed concrete legs, the elevated horizontal form is made up of rhomboids and triangles, and resembles an enormous origami snake. It was designed and built in only three weeks. Everything about the visitor's experience is chocolate-themed, with chocolate-bar-shaped sofas in the reception and chocolate-chunk-shaped cushions to sit on in the auditorium. When the children have wound their way past various exhibits, they're ready for the climax of the tour: the factory visit. Entering by tunnel, they can watch (and smell) the delicious confectionery being made. Afterwards, returning of course via the enormous gift shop, they can buy as much chocolate as they can eat. As Nestlé's brand color, red was the obvious choice for the museum's exterior—it's clad in a striking, corrugated scarlet steel.

Coca-Cola Beatbox Pavilion | **Asif Khan and Pernilla Ohrstedt**
London, England, UK
2012

The clack of a ping-pong ball, the squeak of sneakers on a gym floor, and the crack of a starting pistol were among the sounds that visitors could conjure to create an interactive sound sculpture in this Coca-Cola-sponsored pavilion designed for the London 2012 Olympics. Created by London-based architects Asif Khan and Pernilla Ohrstedt, the structure was in Coca-Cola's unmistakable red and white colors. It was made of 200 interlocking plastic EFTE (Ethylene tetrafluoroethylene) pillows, each embedded with a different sound recording, which, when touched or waved at, could be played like a musical instrument. The sounds were sampled from Mark Ronson and Katy B's track "Anywhere In The World"—and the pillows also included light sensors, creating a visual as well as sonic experience. The spiky, nest-like pavilion was about 115 feet (35 meters) in diameter and visitors explored the space via a sloping, spiraling walkway. The architects had been selected as the "best of emerging British talent": Khan had previously designed the West Beach Café at Littlehampton and Ohrstedt the Canadian Pavilion at the 2010 Venice Architecture Biennale. The architects' first joint commission had been to design a range of furniture made of flowers, called Harvest. They described their ambition as being "to test the limits of people's imaginations and introduce new ways of seeing things."

Ragnarock/Rock Museum | **MVRDV & COBE**
Roskilde, Denmark
2016

Ragnarock, a joint project between a Dutch and a Danish architectural practice, serves a unique function as Denmark's museum for pop, rock, and youth culture—its name stemming from its location among a collection of disused concrete factory buildings on the outskirts of Copenhagen. While regal, its golden-studded facade—which wraps around to highlight a grand cantilever, protruding by 65 feet (20 meters)—says little of its glamorous, velvety crimson interior. The language of the facade extends inside by means of a red carpet. Here, studded wall panels combined with a gleaming, mirrored floor make a statement about the historically defiant, and at times controversial, nature of rock music. The building, defined by its bold color scheme, exudes a contemporary energy at the same time as referring to local folklore. *Ragnarök*, the legendary Norse "Doom of the Gods," spoke of the disastrous events that would lead to the almost total destruction of humanity. While undoubtedly less cataclysmic in tone than the mythology might suggest, Ragnarock loosely refers to the rise and demise of a, or all, rock stars; visitors ascend to fame, whereupon they reach an auditorium before being invited to make an "inevitable descent" to the museum's bar.

MK-CK5 Production Office | **Agaligo Studio**
| **Mueang Samut, Thailand**
| **2013**

MK Restaurants are a hugely successful brand in Thailand, a business that has been running for over half a century. From humble origins, they have grown to a chain of over 250 restaurants. MK serve *suki*—hotpots of fresh meat and vegetables cooked in boiling broth at the table, then dipped in a range of sauces. MK were the first to use electric *suki* pots, which are safer than gas versions; they also introduced space-saving, bright-red stacking serving trays called "condos." "Our brand is to make people feel 'warm;' to give them a warm, pleasant experience," CEO and company founder Rit Thirakomen has said. MK celebrated becoming a public company in 2013 by building a brand new complex which includes a central kitchen, CK5, where food is freshly prepared; new offices; and a visitor experience. The architect's concept was called "Red Boxes on the Move," inspired by MK's condo trays. The three-storey red office building suggest the stacking condos, twisting at the first and second floors to create a sense of dynamism and innovation. The office's red aluminium cladding was matched carefully to the exact shade of the MK condo. Landscaping nearby includes a pool in the shape of a *suki* pot, lined with digitally designed hexagonal tiling to resemble the forms of boiling vegetables. Inside, meeting-room walls are made of glass with a white gradient pattern suggesting the steam rising from a *suki*.

Red Guest Houses | **Totan Kuzembaev**
Klyazminskoye Reservoir, Russia
2003

The Pirogovo resort near Moscow is now a private, high-end bolt-hole for the wealthy, but this wasn't always the case. It was ordered to be built in 1960 by Nikita Khrushchev, leader of the Soviet Union from 1955 to 1964, in a watery, marshy area around Bukhta Radosti Bay, a system of waterways built by gulag prisoners to connect the Volga and Moskva rivers. In 2002, its new owner, Alexander Ezhkov, decided to rebuild the resort: the beaches were overcrowded, full of rubbish, and dotted with the remains of tourist campfires. Ezhkov commissioned well-known architects Alexandr Brodsky, Nikolai Lyzlov, and Totan Kuzembaev to create an altogether more exclusive complex. Kuzembaev designed the very first homes to be built—the red

weekend cabins that have now become symbols of Pirovogo. The cabins' architecture is designed to suit the landscape, to be futuristic without being high-tech. The huts are boat-shaped, built on stilts, and have large semi-circular balconies overlooking the lake. Their style, including the red color, is influenced by Constructivism in its powerful geometry and strong diagonal line, but the huts also reference traditional Russian wooden house-building. Each home is a compact 387 square feet (36 square meters) in area, with one bedroom. The staircases leading up to the living levels are covered in oblique wooden fins, which make more abstract forms.

Water Temple | **Tadao Ando Architects and Associates**
Awaji–Shima, Japan
1991

The Water Temple, designed by the world-renowned Japanese architect Tadao Ando, is located on Awaji Island, in Hyōgo Prefecture. Designed originally by the Shingon Buddhists, the building embodies an accomplished constellation of worlds, ideas, and rituals. From the outside, the building is tranquil: partially embedded in the landscape and defined by a boldly simple arrangement of two curved concrete walls, the structure gathers round a large, circular pool of still water. Reflections of the surrounding mountains, paddy fields, forests, and groves define its position in what might be perceived as an infinite horizon. Visitors descend a staircase into, and under, the reflecting pool. In contrast to the neutral purity of its exterior, the interior is flooded with color—an acute, bright vermillion. Here, the most sacred spaces of the temple appear to pulsate with light and intensity: a contemplative sanctuary of profound stillness. The color of these internal spaces peaks at sunset. A large west-facing window allows western light (which has a particular significance in Buddhist temples because Siddhārtha Gautama—the Buddha—came from what is now India) to flood the internal spaces at close of day. For those who visit, the experience of light, color, and gestural movement embodied by this temple is spiritual.

Autostella Showroom | **Supermachine Studio**
Bangkok, Thailand
| **2009**

The relationship between car design and architecture has been widely discussed. When the notion of modern utopias took hold in the early twentieth century, spearheaded by figures such as Le Corbusier, the motorcar symbolized the likely future: efficient, streamlined, and mechanical. Architecture responded accordingly. Today, though, the bridge between the industries is more a gulf. In Bangkok, the Autostella Showroom—a small-scale, imported-car showroom—seeks to reestablish this now historic relationship. Housing a number of Italian cars, the showroom rejects the now-common large, curtain-wall glazing of this type of structure. It's more domestic in scale and, importantly for its character, is rendered, externally a flashy, fiery red.

The volume of the building—a series of trapezoid spaces, merged as one—projects toward the adjacent highway. Large windows showcase some of the vehicles; they appear as residents rather than products for sale. In the words of the architects, the building has been designed like a small café or bakery, eschewing all sense of a large, empty warehouse that car showrooms so often give. Inside, the building is largely white and designed carefully in order not to feel hollow. Colored lights—yellow, orange, and red—imbue the rooms with a sense of comforting homeliness. Rather than simply buying a car, Autostella want their customers to buy into a car: in this, the architecture is instrumental.

242 Social-Housing Units | **IDOM**
Salburúa, Spain
2011

Five apartment blocks in a row, like a fleet of urban battleships, create a dramatic skyline in Salburúa. A residential district has been developed here on the site of drained wetlands, close to a park of lakes, meadows, and woodlands. As part of Salburúa's expansion process, the city council wanted to create a recognizable cityscape, hence its commissioning this series of apartment blocks. One block of the five, in the middle, is even more prominent: these vivid-red social-housing units are a landmark within a landmark. The red of the block is, according to the architects, meant to stand for "optimism, confidence, and commitment to the future." Its twenty-storey tower sits on top of a U-shaped block of four to seven storeys, built around a landscaped courtyard. It includes nine retail units. All the apartments are double-fronted, so that bedrooms overlook the courtyard garden and the living spaces overlook the street. The height of the building allows maximum sunlight to reach the courtyard and the balconies of every apartment. Energy has been carefully considered in this project. As well as having a conventional boiler, the complex has its own cogeneration unit. Powered by natural gas, the unit generates both heat and electricity from its own carbon dioxide emissions, reducing residents' bills and creating a surplus to sell back to energy suppliers.

China Art Museum | He Jingtang
Shanghai, China
2010

A building of many superlatives, the China Art Museum is the largest art museum in Asia. It has a previous life, albeit a brief one, as the Chinese Pavilion at the World Expo 2010. Built on the east bank of the Huangpu River in Shanghai, this was the largest of all the national pavilions—in fact, it was the largest in the history of the World Expo fairs. The Shanghai Expo was future-focused and was part of a wider plan to develop new city quarters; the Chinese Pavilion was to be the flagship building of a new museum and cultural district. Known as the "Oriental Crown," the Expo building had two clear components: the red rooftop of the China National Pavilion and the ivory podium of the provincial regions. All this has now been subsumed into the art museum. The roof is supported by four massive pillars, which act as service and transportational cores. It uses the traditional Chinese *dougong* brackets—where *dou* means "cap" and *gong* means "block"—to support its crossbeams. Its landscaping is particularly sympathetic, creating a green oasis in built-up Shanghai, with grasses, waterways, and trees that work in harmony with the color of the building. Five floors of art space now host travelling exhibitions and a mainly modern art collection.

Harvey Pediatric Clinic | **Marlon Blackwell**
Rogers, Arkansas, USA
2016

When it comes to wellness and healthcare, color can play a surprisingly significant part during a patient's treatment and recovery. At the Harvey Pediatric Clinic in Rogers, Arkansas, such thoughts are put into practice. In a context once defined by industrial architecture—barns, silos, and garages—this building stands apart. Bold in form, the project is also defiant and brash: against a sea of gray and beige, this clinic is wrapped on one side in cayenne-colored sheet metal, marking the main entrance. Inside, the spaces are white and tinted with blue light by way of a skylight. The relationship between blue (inside) and red (outside) enables a dramatic shift in mood and tone; from a distance, the building is keenly identifiable and more

tranquil within. At one end of the building is a wall of windows protected from direct sunlight by a wall of deep fins. The inner linings of these are also colored red, representing the only indication of the building's exterior character visible from inside. This project benefits from a strikingly simple but intelligently conceived influence of the color spectrum on an individual's subconscious well-being.

"Red is the ultimate cure for sadness."

Bill Blass | **Fashion Designer (1922–2002)**

"Red is the ultimate cure for sadness."

Red Building, Pacific Design Center | **Pelli Clarke Pelli**
Los Angeles, California, USA
2012

A group of abstract, gargantuan shapes huddle at the corner of Melrose Avenue and San Vicente Boulevard, West Hollywood. The Pacific Design Center is a landmark—a one-stop shop for the interior design trades, filled with lighting, wall hangings, fabrics, and floor coverings. Anything you need for a home, you can buy here. The complex has been designed by César Pelli over four decades. Blue Building, also known as the "Blue Whale," opened in 1975; the Green Building followed in 1988, and finally the Red Building was completed in 2012. The buildings are grouped around a 14-acre (5.6-hectare) plaza and include space for exhibitions, events, and conferences, plus a 294-seat luxury cinema and two restaurants. Pelli conceived them as gigantic fragments of some unknown planets, or space junk that's fallen to earth. The Red Building looks like a warped cruise liner. A gigantic 797,000 square feet (74,000 square meters) in area, its sweeping prow lurches forward, supported on pillars. It comprises two towers on top of seven floors of parking. The West Tower is five storeys tall and slopes inwards, to the north; the East Tower has eight storeys and curves upwards towards the east. On the eighth floor, a palm-fringed courtyard is a light-filled disruption between the two red volumes. Like the other two buildings in the group, the Red Building is clad in transparent, fritted (finely porous) glass. To create a taut appearance, it's held with silicone in aluminum frames.

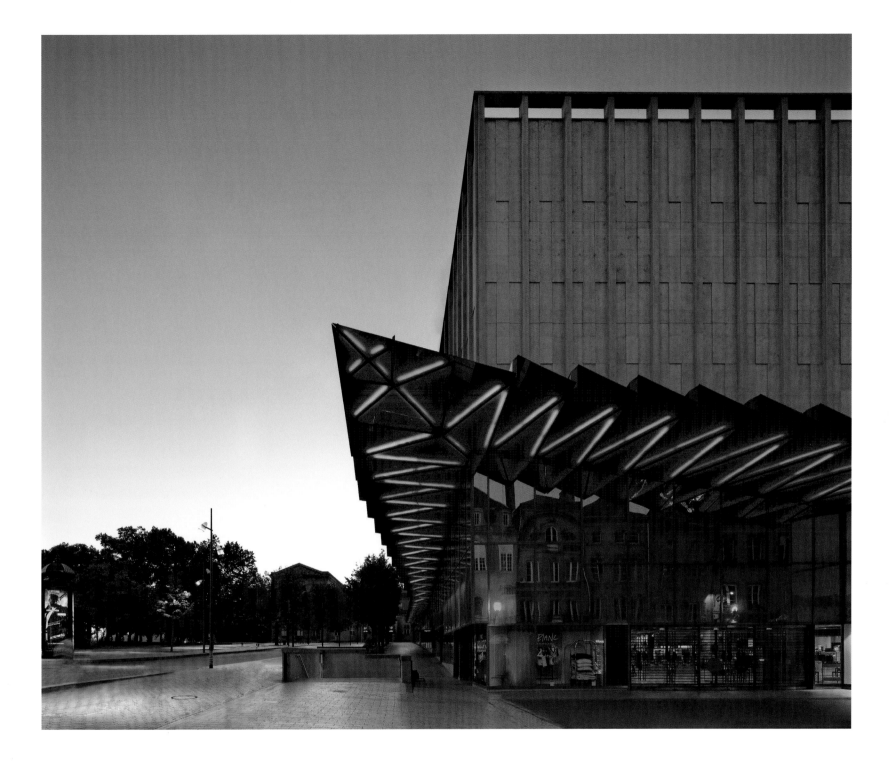

Galeries Lafayette, Metz | **Manuelle Gautrand Architecture**
Metz, France
2014

After three decades of trading, the Metz branch of department store Galeries Lafayette needed a revamp, and commissioned Manuelle Gautrand for an external refurbishment. The store was well known for its minimalist and sombre stone-covered, windowless facade, and that was to remain. Gautrand therefore focused on designing a 394-foot (120-meter) glass canopy to create a dramatic new identity for the store, transforming it into an unmissable city center landmark. The choice of glass was, says Gautrand, an homage to the tradition of glassmaking in Alsace–Lorraine since medieval times (Lalique and Baccarat both originate from the region). Resembling a monumental length of pleated red fabric, the canopy runs along three sides of the building, zigzagging in and out of the ridges of stone, swooping dramatically upward at the shop's corners. Each pleat's depth varies from 7 feet 6 inches to 17 feet (2.3 meters to 5.2 meters), culminating in an impressive 24-foot (7.3-meter) cantilever over the Place de la République, which signposts the store's entrance. Below the canopy, a new section of mirrored glass has been added to open up the storefront and illuminate the ground floor. The vibrant lighting of the glass, by the design agency ON, creates a warm glow on the stone building itself, causing it to turn a subtle shade of red.

Red Dot Design Museum | **Frank Dorrington Ward**
Singapore
1928

When it was completed in the late 1920s, the building that now houses the Red Dot Design Museum was a police barracks. From the moment it was opened, the building was a beacon, a local icon. Designed by the Straits Settlements' Public Works Department's chief architect, Frank Dorrington Ward, the building accommodated the traffic police, and was the place every citizen went when taking their driving test. This building, therefore, symbolized, for many, a rite of passage. In 2005, following six years of being empty, it was repurposed as a design museum and creative hub—and painted a deep crimson. The building, in the rather orthodox architectural style of a colonial office, reclaimed its place in local hearts following this transformation. Known for its heritage and striking cloak of red, controversy surrounded the museum in 2017 when the protected building was mooted for a new facade—this time, off-white—all in the name of restoration. It demonstrates that for some, the importance of the color of a building often goes deeper than a coat of paint.

Archipel Theater | **Jean Nouvel**
Perpignan, France
2011

The Archipel Theater, located on Perpignan's Avenue Général Leclerc, is a symphony in shades of red. Comprising a motley assortment of large spatial volumes, the material expression of the building is just as diverse. From Cor-Ten (a steel, the surface of which rusts controllably) to pink-pigmented concrete, sheet metal to glossy garnet render, the building communicates in multiple materials simultaneously. Intended to represent Catalan culture, it is apt, perhaps, that it speaks of overlapping identities and pluralism: a character that many cultural projects of its scale and scope ignore. On the banks of the Tet River, this was—and remains—a controversial scheme. Those who read it as a building, however, might be missing the point:

this theater—or agglomeration of theaters—more accurately, represents a crossroads of performance, from ballet and opera to modern dance and classical music. Its color, also, goes further than its envelope might at first suggest. In a scale model of the project, the architects presented the larger of its auditoria—the big red blob—as a gemstone, reflecting and refracting the light of the community that surrounds it. This ambition, while lofty, represents the deeper meaning behind this center: that culture thrives if it's visible and bright.

The House in the Clouds | **G.S. Ogilvie, F. Forbes Glennie**
Thorpeness, England, UK
1923

In 1910, Scottish architect, barrister, and playwright Glencairn Stuart Ogilvie acquired a small hamlet in Suffolk with the dream of creating Thorpeness—a utopian holiday village for his family and friends. Drawing on ideas of "Merrie England"—a sterotype of the rural idyll—it would eventually have mock-Tudor cottages, a hand-dug shallow lake for children (complete with islands inspired by *Peter Pan* by J.M. Barrie), and its own railway station. The village needed a water supply, so a 50,000-gallon (227,000-liter) water tower was constructed by the Braithwaite Engineering Company of London in 1923. Unfortunately, the 70-foot (21-meter) tower was a blot on the idyllic landscape of Thorpeness. With architect Frederick Forbes Glennie, Ogilvie designed what resembled a fairytale cottage to sit at the top of the tower, transforming its prosaic functionality into something magical. The tower was still supplying the village until 1963, when it got its own mains supply; thereafter it was used only for water storage. After the liquidation of Thorpeness Estates in 1977, the whole village fell into private ownership. Interior renovation began in 1987, while the tower's exterior was renovated up to the early 2000s. Children's book author Mrs Malcolm Mason christened it "the house in the clouds," and it's now rented out as holiday accommodation.

Brembo Technical Center | **Jean Nouvel**
Bergamo, Italy
2002

At the edge of the motorway connecting Milan to Venice through Lombardy and the Po Valley, this technical center is the research offices and workshops of Brembo—a company dedicated to high-end automative disc-brake technology. Red is an apt color: the brake light, the stop sign. Its architects conceived a just over one-and-a-half-mile- (one-kilometer-) long structure in response to the company's brief: vivid red, and visible for miles. The *Kilometro Rosso*, as it is known locally, is made of lacquered aluminum. Its grooved facade glints in the sunlight, echoing the age—and the future—of speed on four wheels. The result, in many ways, is less a building, more a wall. Behind it, on the other side of the busy motorway, is a muddle of industrial buildings—functional rather than aesthetic. This wall is a sound barrier, keeping the roar of engines out of the technical rooms and allowing for the creation of peaceful parklands around it. The red line bisects the countryside around it, reframing it entirely. The boldest gestures are often the best.

2 Sisters House | **NRJA**
Riga, Latvia
2007

Langstini Lake, located to the northeast of Riga, Latvia, is a popular place for locals to get away from it all. This simple, compact development, designed by Riga-based practice NRJA (standing for No Rules Just Architecture), was built for two families who wanted to have homes next to one another while retaining some privacy. Each house is 3,610 square feet (335.4 square meters) in area; the two dwellings share a common space on the ground floor, but upstairs each is completely self-contained. In both houses, the upper floors are supported on concrete pillars that echo the elegant forms of the surrounding trees. The two units are arranged in a V-formation, with one house slightly further forward than the other; both houses have

expansive terraces for making the most of the view. The panoramic glazing is met with a beautiful screen of trees, and, through the leaves, the blue of the lake can be glimpsed. The facades are wood-clad, and painted a pillar-box red, giving the homes a delightful sense of warmth and sociability. In spring and summer, the red seems luminous against the greens of leaves and grass; in winter, it looks phenomenal in the pure-white snow.

Sjakket Youth Club | **PLOT = BIG + JDS**
Copenhagen, Denmark
2007

Contemporary Danish architecture is known for its playful approach to spatial design, and the Sjakket Youth Club on the outskirts of Copenhagen exemplifies this. A dilapidated industrial space turned base camp for immigrant youth, the intention of the project is to provide an alternative to the streets as a place to meet, with, among other things, a large-scale sports hall. Much of the outside of the building is subject to strict regulations for preservation. With this in mind, the spectacular red-lined spaces were given sensitive new leases of life through the use of color and light. As a result, and from the outside, the square windows become important indicators of the building's renewed function. Bright green and red tints create an unmissable attraction from the street and reflect bright colors within. At the top of the building, a vast container-like structure is accessible by outdoor staircases from a hidden roof terrace. A strikingly contemporary intervention, this structure is lined on one side with floor-to-ceiling windows, signifying the open attitude to which the center aspires.

Baeken Woensel-West | **Bas Termeer**
Eindhoven, The Netherlands
2015

Conceived as part of the Woensel-West Wedstrijd ideas competition in 2011, Baeken Woensel-West has become symbolic of the "Super Dutch" style. Described by its architects as a "problem area" of the eastern city of Eindhoven, the house forms part of a string of sixteen iconic buildings occupying the corners of a single street. Its site marks the edge of a square known as the city's red-light district. On a heavy gray plinth, the structure proper ascends upward in a cuboid form rendered bright red. Inside are two short-stay hotel rooms, surrounded by a separate steel volume clad in a lace-like ornamental netting—"a giant fishnet stocking." This secondary volume, while serving little function, outlines the shape of a prototypical pitched-roof house. In the words of the architects, these two elements—"volume and voile"—create an intricate relationship; those of the introvert and extrovert. On one side of the building, a bright-red staircase ascends the exterior of the internal volume, connecting the hotel rooms with an elevated outdoor terrace.

Espaço 180 | **Penique Productions**
Lisbon, Portugal
2013

This striking installation was created for the Festival of Innovation and Creativity, located at Lisbon's Parque das Nacoes between 1 and 17 November 2013. A series of glossy, conjoined, inflated tubes twisted and turned in a simple spiral arrangement, the structure's form was dictated by a carefully arranged swathe of 26-feet- (8-meter-) high white flagpoles. The empty skin of the inflatable was then arranged within this pattern and filled with air. The white poles provided a striking chromatic contrast with the red sculpture, resembling gigantic pins that threatened to puncture the inflatable's playful rotundity. The installation offered two maze-like routes to explore: a path around the exterior's bulging forms or—more interestingly—an internal route providing a womb-like and contemplative space where the semi-transparent walls allowed light and color to constantly shift and flow. Visitors followed the labyrinth to its center, where they encountered a mysteriously inaccessible, veiled space. The blood-red hue, the tubal structures, and the fragile membrane walls created an experience suggestive of walking inside a giant organic body. The structure's ephemerality was its key. Penique Productions, the company behind it, is a collective established in Barcelona in 2007, specializing in customised, site-specific temporary installations. Are they containers, art objects, or buildings? They are probably all three.

Herstal City Hall | **Frederic Haesevoets Architecte**
Herstal, Belgium
2015

Herstal is a city of around 600,000 inhabitants in Liège Province. An open competition was held to find an architect to design a new townhall complex for the municipality. Frederic Haesevoets won with an audacious proposal for two huge volumes housing the main office areas in "a techno-sensual wrapping," connected by a bright-red bridge. Efficiency, transparency, and innovation were the values that the architects wanted to convey. The administrative campus accommodates offices, a council chamber, meeting rooms, archives, outdoor public spaces, and car parking. The two volumes' faceted facades feature real trees inserted between the panes of glass, to make being in an office a more natural, organic experience. Color was used thoughtfully in the design of the complex, with bright tones not usually associated with administration buildings. Red denotes a circulation space (working spaces are green, common spaces gray, and technical spaces blue). The connecting walkway between the two wings is red on the outside, therefore creating a dazzling contrast with the green of the trees embedded into the facade, and is also red on the inside, as are all the other corridors, lobbies, and vestibules in the building. LED lighting enhances staircases, adding a warm, positive glow. Stair balustrades are in translucent red Perspex, a literal way of adding to the building's perceived transparency. The city hall is a bold symbol of sustainability, new ways of working, and optimism.

PaperBridge | **Steve Messam**
Lake District, England, UK
2015

PaperBridge, in the English Lake District, is an artwork of and for its open, natural context. Supported end-to-end by two gabions (cages filled with stones, rocks, or concrete), it is a play on structure and physics—built entirely of locally produced sheets of paper (wood pulp and water). Compressed and carefully shaped, the resulting footbridge is remarkably strong and connects two paths that meet at the banks of a gently flowing beck (stream), communicating the fundamental nature of the landscape that it sits in. While the shape of the bridge is familiar, it's aesthetically charged. The vibrant red of the material is a focal point in the valley. Undulating fields and sloping hillsides, broken only by snaking drystone walls, all appear to lead to

the *PaperBridge*. It draws the gaze, as would a tree on a tundra, to interfere with the natural order of the terrain. Its symbolic presence as an architectural element plays with existing sightlines while creating new ones, playing with conceptions of non-agricultural countryside. This bridge could not exist elsewhere: a wayfinding landmark and visual challenge in one.

"Red is one of the strongest colors, it's blood, it has a power with the eye. That's why traffic lights are red I guess, and stop signs as well ... In fact I use red in all of my paintings."

Keith Haring | **Artist (1958–1990)**

Fire Department Headquarters and Training School | **BFM Architects**
Cologne, Germany
2007

This bright-red, latticed concrete ring surrounds Cologne's central fire station. Here, emergency calls are processed and sent out to different fire brigades around the city; there is also an in-house team of firefighters. Four storeys high, the upper floors of the building are devoted to the call center and management offices. On the ground floor are the rescue vehicles and additional rooms for training and services, and accommodation for on-duty firefighters. The fire station has been designed in such a way that the call-center area can be expanded easily if necessary. Inside, floor-to-ceiling glazing in many places creates a much lighter and brighter space than the fire services' previous headquarters. An abstract flame pattern created by the external lattice frames the views out. Connected to the drum is a block-shaped four-storey building, reached by a glass-covered bridge, which is used for training the fire and emergency services personnel. Landscaping around the ring helps create an atmosphere of well-being. It's unusual for a city to commission such an audacious, eye-catching center for its emergency rescue services.

Château de la Dominique | **Jean Nouvel**
Saint-Emilion, France
2014

Having recently expanded in size, the vineyard Château de la Dominique in Saint-Emilion commissioned Jean Nouvel to create a new fermenting room and cellar to complement its existing buildings. The focus of the estate was a two-storey Classical mansion. Surrounding this are two parallel wings, forming a U shape; Nouvel designed the new extension within this space, abutting the older building. A long, low orthogonal structure, it's enveloped in an astonishingly minimalist cladding of mirrored red, stainless-steel blades in six different shades of the color, to reflect the various hues of red wine. The blades incline gently upwards to catch the maximum reflection of the surrounding vineyards. Inside this structure is the 6,458-square-foot (600-square-meter) vat room, full of state-of-the-art fermenting equipment, illuminated by a gigantic bay window. The space has been designed to host events such as professional wine tastings, with the roof terrace providing fantastic panoramic views over the Saint-Emilion vineyards. The terrace features a small square filled with red glass pebbles, which the visitor can, symbolically, walk across, referencing the old method of treading grapes. Where the new building meets the stone wall of the old, the space is used for storing wine in oak casks until it matures.

Glass House | **Philip Johnson, Yayoi Kusama (installation)**
New Canaan, Connecticut, USA
2016

In this month-long installation, the artist Yayoi Kusama covered Philip Johnson's famous glass house in Connecticut with bright-red dots. Part of a wider series of works called *Narcissus Garden*, Kusama's decoration of the house was entitled *Dots Obsession—Alive, Seeking for Eternal Hope*. Kusama, Japan's most prominent contemporary artist, is known for using polka dots (notably for painting naked participants with multi-colored dots in the late 1960s). She has called her vast fields of polka dots "infinity nets." Philip Johnson's Miesian Glass House was built by the architect in 1949 in a beautiful, green, 49-acre (20-hectare) estate. Now a National Trust historic site, it hosts exhibitions and art installations. Johnson admired Kusama's work, so

it was entirely fitting that she was invited to create an installation to commemorate what would have been his 110th birthday (he died in 2005). Johnson's house also plays with ideas of infinity; the opening up of endless, shifting perspectives. The red dots were distributed across every part of the glass elevations, disrupting the boundless views and—almost sacrilegiously—the home's minimalism—but they created new ways of perceiving space, and new ways of looking. For Kusama, the polka dots suggest being part of a greater network, a sense of connectivity. They turned Johnson's meditative but shrine-like space into something alive with energy, full of hope and possibility—and he surely would have loved that.

2MS Series No. 1 | **Bernard Schottlander**
Milton Keynes, England, UK
1970

Milton Keynes, one of the so-called British "new towns" in 1967, was developed over the late 1960s and 1970s to alleviate London's chronic housing shortage and provide a commercial center for Buckinghamshire. Gently mocked for its uniformity and endless interlinking roundabouts, a surprising amount of avant-garde sculpture was commissioned for the town, including this by Bernard Schottlander. Born to a Jewish family in 1924, Schottlander fled Nazi Germany, settling in Leeds in 1939, training as a welder and later studying sculpture. He was also an industrial designer, and is perhaps best known for his Mantis lamp, inspired by Alexander Calder's work. Milton Keynes' brave new world of modern buildings and empty green landscaping provided the perfect backdrop for Schottlander's enigmatic, abstract sculptures. *2MS Series No. 1* is located within the grounds of Challenge House (then named Sherwood House), a business center. It's an impressive 27 feet 6 inches (8.4 meters) long, and consists of two sections of bright-red, mild steel. The trapezoidal, fluted forms meet at a single point; the larger piece rests improbably on the smallest of bases. The sculpture was Grade II listed by English Heritage for its special architectural and historic interest in 2016. Three other Schottlander pieces were commissioned as public art for the town—*3B Series No. 2*, *3B Series No. 6*, and *2MS Series No. 4*.

Red Barn | **Roger Ferris and Partners**
Connecticut, USA
2016

On the Connecticut coast, Red Barn houses an artist's home and studio. Defined by a conventional volume—that of a pitched-roof home—the simplicity of the building's exterior belies a more layered series of openings. From afar, it appears as a solid red structure, without any perceptible windows or doors. In reality, one gable end of the structure is entirely glazed, disguised by red louvers. A sophisticated fiber-cement composite material was used to shroud the building in color, from the walls to the roof. This forms a continuous surface of sorts, lending the structure a monolithic quality. With an almost pearlescent character, the facade shimmers in the light while reflecting—and, at times, absorbing—shadows from nearby trees.

Inside, the color scheme dissolves to a neutral white. Here, minimal living is the order of the day; with a working studio and workshop on the first floor, living areas are positioned on the second. Strikingly simple, Red Barn is a contemporary interpretation of New England's vernacular heritage.

Salmtal Secondary School Canteen | **Spreier Trenner Architekten**
Salmtal, Germany
2012

The canteen at this secondary school in Salmtal, Germany, is designed with flexibility in mind. Unassuming in scale and shape, the building is used daily by schoolchildren, but also serves as a makeshift theater, concert venue, and location for community fairs. Inside it is a free space—in other words, no structural columns divide the room, although a mobile wall can be used to isolate certain areas as and when required. Externally, the facade makes use of a geometric pattern of interwoven panels. Some are occupied by windows, while others are red panels. This logic translates inside, where the same pattern is evident on both the walls and in the ceiling, which is an entirely structural two-directional grid. This is, therefore, a building in which structure reigns supreme; it becomes a design motif. In the words of the architects, the "surrounding landscape is able to appear like pictures hung on the wall." For children, this building has a comforting coherence; it is able to use minimal design gestures to create a space full of interaction. Its colored facade ensures it remains recognizable and familiar.

Red House | **JVA**
Oslo, Norway
2011

On the banks of a wooded river valley in the suburbs of Oslo, Red House is a dramatic, multi-level home with views across the surrounding landscape and a canopy of tall trees. Orthogonal in shape, defined by harsh edges and clean lines, the house also has—perhaps unsurprisingly, given its external character—a logical, context-oriented spatial arrangement. With two floors of living spaces, the building makes the most of its unique position by way of views and vistas; large windows bring light inside while reflecting the dense forest beyond. The facade of the house is rendered a striking red; in an area largely defined by postwar family housing, most of which are single dwellings rather than blocks, this building stands out as a beacon of color. The red exterior, typical of wood-clad houses in the Nordic region, is here made brighter and more intense—so it is even more vivid against the snow. The front door and window frames are painted in a slightly darker hue, creating a subtle interplay between shades, contrasting with the greens, browns, and silver birches of the surrounding woodland.

Red Object | **3GATTI**
| **Shanghai, China**
| **2006**

This egg-shaped, multifaceted pod designed by Rome- and Shanghai-based 3GATTI is a two-storey unit housing two meeting rooms and a kitchen. This sculptural oddity was part of a wider brief to convert a former factory in Jing An, Shanghai, into offices. In the process, the architects took the double-height space and added two mezzanine floors joined by two bridge-corridors, creating a central void where the Red Object could be inserted. They also covered much of the factory's concrete interior in white resin, and created a reception area. Francesco Gatti cites red and black as traditionally avant-garde colors, and white, he says, suggests a void or vacuum—all three symbolic of generating something from nothing

with cutting-edge creativity. The Object's main structure is concrete and brick, covered with a secondary wooden layer. It's enveloped in a plasterboard skin with plexiglass openings. Its color and irregularity creates an arresting contrast with the smooth white floors, gray concrete, and open empty space of the offices. The Object is also a place apart—a bright, playful space to meet and brainstorm, somewhere to go for refreshment and even a place to hide, for a while, from office activity. The double-height pod can be accessed either from the ground floor or from a bridge on the mezzanine floor. Its "otherness" adds a new dynamic to the conventional open-plan office.

Touch of Evil | **NIO Architecten**
Pijnacker, The Netherlands
2004

In Pijnacker, a residential suburb of the Dutch city of Rotterdam, *Touch of Evil* intelligently brings a crossroads to life by the simplest means. The site comprises a railway bridge spanning a road, a pedestrian path, and a cycle track: a desolate piece of urban infrastructure which, to most people, would not constitute an exciting urban node. But the bleakest of spots can spur the most interesting forms of creativity. Cast from concrete, this urban installation plays with the malleability of the material by warping and repressing the wall and coloring it a bold, bright shade of red. This installation, which was thoughtfully integrated into the project from the outset, forges a vibrant talking point on people's routes across the flat Dutch landscape

in which hills and slopes—or recesses and rises—are scarce. Described by its architects as "enigmatic" and "unexpected," the project transforms a moment of urban transit with an infusion of color, spurring imaginations and demonstrating that even the smallest of gaps can provide a home for something vibrant and joyful.

Pr34 House | **Rojkind Architects**
Techamachalco, Mexico
2003

Perched on a hillside in Techamachalco on the western edge of Mexico City, this is an imaginative transformation of a simple one-storey 1960s house with pitched roof into a flexible home for a family. The existing building was gutted to improve its spatial configuration. The clients then decided the renovation should include a luxury, self-contained apartment for their daughter—so a design was drawn up for a whole new contemporary structure to be grafted onto the roof of the older house, creating an additional split-level dwelling. On plan, the apartment consists of two pod-like units in staggered formation, with a total floor area of 1,464 square feet (136 square meters). The sensuously curved corners of the pods give the

home a retro, sci-fi feel. The apartment has its own entrance from the garage on the ground floor, and is accessed via a spiral staircase climbing two storeys. It's generously proportioned, with an open-plan seating and dining area, and kitchen, T.V. room, master bedroom, dressing room, and bathroom. Like the hull of a ship, the building's skin is made from steel hammered into shape by workers at repair yards. Its vibrant scarlet tone makes it stand out among the drab buildings and green vegetation of the hillside.

Rockaway! | **Katharina Grosse**
| **Fort Tilden, New York State, USA**
| **2016–17**

Designed by German artist Katharina Grosse, *Rockaway!* was part of the internationally renowned PS1 project by New York's Museum of Modern Art. In an aquatics building at Fort Tilden, a former U.S. Army installation in the borough of Queens, the project makes use of a specialized technique of spray painting. Covering the structure in bright red and white, thereby finding every shade in-between, the artwork sought to monumentalize the ordinary and provide a "final celebration and memorialization" of a locally iconic building rendered structurally unsound by the effects of Hurricane Sandy in 2012. Grosse's use of reds and whites signals a specific statement about color in connection with buildings. When color is considered as

a material, like brick or steel, it's capable of having a profound impact on the ways in which we perceive the built environment. Finding the nuances between light and shadow is challenging on a two-dimensional surface. However, when the surface is extended beyond the scope of four walls and a roof to the scale of a landscape, the gesture of color is made all the more radiant.

Bluub | **Ines Camacho and Isabelle Cornet**
Brussels, Belgium
2010

A submarine-like pod floating on a giant pedestal, Bluub is an unusual mobile classroom: a space to help young children learn about architecture, cities, and planning. The tiny, cocooned space somehow incorporates a projection room, music laboratory, and teaching areas. It has its own water supply and toilets, and the fun interior is designed to get kids thinking about the towns and cities of the future. Scrambling up into Bluub by ladder, children can view their townscape through portholes and a giant, cyclopean, glass window, and are given a new perspective on their environment. Discussions on what makes an ideal town and games about mobility, housing, and energy supply help children to reflect on the urban environment. Bluub was the brainchild of Ines Camacho and Isabelle Cornet. It featured in the Smart Urban Stage festival, which toured European cities in 2010. At 258 square feet (24 square meters) in area, the structure is made of polyester resin, insulated with polystyrene, and has a scarlet steel outer shell. The pedestal is made of concrete and steel to ensure stability. A simple kit of parts, it weighs 5 tonnes, and can be transported to new locations by truck, needing just two hours for assembly.

Flex-Red | **Cerejeira Fontes Architects**
Gualtar, Portugal
2008

The climate of Portugal is, during the summer months at least, typified by sun-drenched days and bright blue skies. In Gualtar, in the northern province of Braga, Flex-Red—a building housing twenty-four apartment buildings in all—appears more vibrant than any of its neighbors. Clad in a perforated, corrugated metal skin, the building's orthodox orthogonal volume belies an intelligent softening of its skin: a layered facade allows the breeze to filter through to sheltered balconies and terraces, while shielding its occupants from the intense heat of day. Everything—from the handrails to, as one might expect, the fire hydrants on the street—are vivid red. Otherwise conventional in design, the facade openings—windows, doors, and balconies—live by the the rhythm of the passing hours. Light and shadow play off the surfaces, allowing all shades of red to appear over the course of a day—from bright white-pinks to gray-toned crimsons. In many ways, Flex-Red could be considered an ordinary building with an extraordinary skin—testament to the idea that what you wear has the potential to shape your mood.

Red Ribbon Park | **Turenscape**
Qinhuangdao, China
2007

A former rubbish dump and abandoned shanty village has been transformed into a park along the Tanghe River in Qinhuangdao. This 547-yard (500-meter) boardwalk, edged by a red, snaking element incorporating lighting and seating, has served not only to create a space for well-being and environmental education but also preserves a large swathe of threatened habitat. The city's inevitable creep outward means the river would probably have been drained and replaced with concrete embankments and ornamental flower beds. Landscape architects Turenscape's clever response to the problem was to create an enticing trail through the green river corridor, given a central identity by this simple, vivid construction. The fiber-steel structure is 24 inches (61 centimeters) high, varying in width, and is connected to a boardwalk. Five cloud-shaped pavilions are placed at intervals, for people to shelter from the sun, to rest, or meet. Previously overgrown areas have been transformed into shady woodlands, vistas of water and islands, and grassy meadows. Bright red is a social and eye-catching color, providing a zesty contrast with the landscape. Used by residents for walking, fishing, jogging, or meditating, this is an example of how a simple idea can improve people's quality of life. As day becomes evening, the space evolves into a beautiful spectacle; lit from within, the ribbon resembles a trail of lava, sending reflections shimmering from the Tanghe.

São Paulo Museum of Art | **Lina Bo Bardi**
São Paulo, Brazil
1968

On São Paulo's Terraço do Trianon, the Museum of Art (known locally as MASP) is an icon in the history of architecture. Its architect was offered the job on condition that under no circumstances should the building mask panoramic views of the city and the nearby public space from the ground. She delivered a remarkably bold solution: to lift the entire interior space fully 26 feet (8 meters) from the ground, by way of a vast bright-red concrete structure. In this, the building allows the continuation of civic space—and, in one way, enhances it with shelter and shade—while providing a large cultural space for the city. Conceived of as a "container for art," the museum has entered the national subconscious—not necessarily for what it exhibits and displays, but for the significance of its color. Here, red signifies an invitation to people—of all and of any background—to take ownership of culture. It is, in other words, a space for the culture of the people. The color continues inside; the staircases, for instance, are also daubed in bright red—suggesting, perhaps, that appropriation is not simply about signifying ownership but also about evoking a willingness to occupy it, too.

"A thimbleful of red is redder than a bucketful."

Henri Matisse | **Painter (1869–1954)**

Kuggen | **Wingårdh Arkitektkontor**
Gothenburg, Sweden
2011

Located in the university district of the Swedish city of Gothenburg, Kuggen is a cylindrical building designed to stimulate and facilitate collaboration between its inhabitants: educators and, primarily, students. Described by its architects as referencing the planning principles of the Italian Renaissance (it boldly occupies a grand, urban square in the same way a sixteenth-century civic structure might), the building is defined first and foremost by an unusually striking, multifaceted, colored facade. A brocade of triangular panels—some pink and some crimson, some orange and some green—skirt the rotunda to create an ordered patchwork of contrasting and complementary pairings; the colors, the architects maintain, reference shades of industrial paint used in the nearby docklands. The facade serves a second function: in order to deal with changing patterns of light, the brocade provides solar shading while also reflecting the sun. Achieving a sense of movement on the outside of the building allows for changing character within; a key ambition behind the interior design of Kuggen is to encourage informal meetings and conversation. Motion-activated mood lighting lends the spaces a sense of continual change and renewal.

The Blue Cone | **SandellSandberg**
Harads, Sweden
2010

The ironically named The Blue Cone (there's nothing blue about it) is one of seven wonder-inducing treehouses in this unique hotel in remote Harads, 31 miles (50 kilometers) south of the Arctic Circle. Established by Kent Lindall and his wife Britta in 2010, the Treehotel features a range of extraordinary tree dwellings, including the Mirrorcube, UFO, Bird's Nest, and The Blue Cone. The couple were struggling to attract guests, and realized they had to come up with a new offering. Inspired by Jonas Selberg Augustsén's film *The Tree Lover*, the story of three city-dwellers who build a treehouse together in the forest, they commissioned seven different architects to entice people to stay—and it's worked brilliantly. Designed by SandellSandberg, The Blue Cone is a simple wooden structure supported by a tripod of three stilts. Downstairs, there's one double bedroom and a tiny living space and bathroom; up a ladder is a portholed mezzanine with two single beds. The tree cabin is designed in simple, primitive house form, with a square base and pyramidal roof, creating a conical shape. Slightly elevated, it's accessible by a gently sloping ramp. Inside, it's painted pure white to maximize the sense of space, and outside, the treehouse's peppy exterior is an oblique, tongue-in-cheek reference to Swedish falu red—but ramped up and much brighter. Is it a forest cabin or a space rocket? It's up to the inhabitants to decide.

Falu Cottages | **Anonymous**
Tjörn, Sweden
1800s

These huts on a waterfront jetty in Hällene, on the west coast island of Tjörn, are painted in falu red, as are many wooden structures in Sweden. "Falurödfärg" originates from the copper mines of Falun, in the province of Darna, which operated from around 1000 to 1992, and supplied up to two-thirds of Europe's copper during this period. In the sixteenth century, it was discovered that when copper and its mining by-products—silica, iron ocher, and zinc—are mixed with linseed oil, the concoction forms a paint. This paint has waterproofing and anti-fungal qualities, and so was used on wooden houses and barns. It was also meant to mimic more expensive brick but, by the seventeenth century, falu red had become fashionable, and was used in the city as well as the country. Falu-red-painted buildings are particularly common in Sweden, but are found throughout Scandinavia. In Finland, for example, it is known as *punamulta* ("red earth") and in the Baltic country Estonia, it's known as *Rootsi punane* ("Swedish red"). Migrants to America from Sweden painted their rural buildings this color, where it's become known as "barn red." So beloved is the color that in 2014, Swedish artist Mikael Genberg attempted to raise $15 million to send a self-assembly house to the moon, specifying that it should be "a typical Swedish cottage"—falu red, with white gables.

The Red Apple | **KCAP Architects and Planners and Jan des Bouvrie**
Rotterdam, The Netherlands
2009

The Red Apple is a smart, mixed-use development with 241 apartments, restaurants, shops, and business spaces in the southwest corner of Rotterdam's Wijnhaven Island. Its name is an obvious reference to New York, but is also a hint at the history of the site: it was here that flat-bottomed boats would unload their cargoes of apples to be sold in local markets. Wijnhaven Island is between Rotterdam's city center and the River Maas, with water on three sides and far-reaching views over the Oude Havven (Old Harbor). The forty-storey development consists of two volumes—a wedge-shaped, cantilevering apartment block and a slender, mixed-use tower. The two entities are connected by a plinth that anchors both into the existing surroundings. All the apartments face diagonally outward to ensure the best views. In both buildings, the extraordinary panoramas call for the maximum amount of glazing. Both volumes are clad with strips of aluminium—running horizontally for the cantilevering block, vertically for the tower—which has been anodized rather than painted to achieve a particular, deep apple-red. On the tower, the red facade strips ripple irregularly up the building—likened by locals to the bending stalks of bamboo. They create an intriguing sense of visual distortion and movement as they are caught by the changing light.

Version Rubis Housing | **Jean-Paul Viguier Architecture**
Montpellier, France
2012

In Montpellier, areas called ZACs—zones d'aménagement concertés, or joint development zones—have been created to respond to a housing shortage in the city. These generally consist of four- or five-storey developments, include local amenities, and are close to public-transport stops. The developments have to conform to various planning regulations, one of which is to be sustainable. Other rules concern the architecture: ZAC blocks have to rest on a concrete podium, and must also have recessed top floors. This assertively bright apartment block is located in the ZAC Parc Marianne, in the east of Montpellier. The emphasis in this development is on quality of life, and housing blocks and amenities are grouped around a generous

17-acre (7-hectare) rectangle of parkland. In the high-end Version Rubis development, architects managed to negotiate considerably more storeys than the usual four or five: the block has ten floors with a south-facing six-floor wing. In addition, there are two luxurious penthouses on the roof occupying two storeys each. Some apartments, instead of having built-in balconies, have terraces projecting at right angles to the building. The L-shaped block is given some complexity with these projecting and recessing volumes. Perforated sunscreens create a rhythmic pattern, while four different shades of red are used in its lacquered aluminium cladding, allowing the block to stand out within the development.

Petersen Automotive Museum | **KPF**
Los Angeles, California, USA
2015

KPF's vibrant refurbishment of the Petersen Automotive Museum has drawn strong reactions, and it is certainly anything but subtle. But then, perhaps, subtlety was never appropriate for a museum celebrating the culture, art, and history of the car in Los Angeles, a city infatuated with the automobile. As part of the upgrade, the existing rectangular building was wrapped in a corrugated aluminium rainscreen, painted Hot Rod red and enveloped by a skin of steel ribbons, sculpted to create the shape of a sports car. The swirling forms give an exuberant sense of speed and movement, but serve no structural purpose. Located on LA's Wilshire Boulevard, the museum is opposite Renzo Piano's LA County Museum of Art. The renovation of the Petersen has created an exhibition space not devoted to any single car brand, but staging a broad exhibition programme to encourage repeat visits. The interior is a brilliant white and red, and continues the sinuous ribbon motif on the ceiling and walls. Despite its critics, the museum has found favor with many: "It's like the old museum crushed down a Redbull and vodka and put on some cool club clothes," said one commentator.

Guizhou Fire Station | **West-line Studio**
| **Gui'an New Area, China**
| **2017**

This sprawling fire station in Gui'an New Area—a suburb of China's "big data" valley, Guiyang—is an exuberant example of how to elevate functional municipal architecture into something spectacular and original. A green, mountainous area, it's developing rapidly as new tech companies move in—a dramatic shift for a previously poor and underdeveloped region. Hugging the hillside, the complex consists of a snow-white central building, enclosed on two sides by two trapezoidal, fire-station-red wings; oblique angles and sloping roofs refer to the topography of the surrounding mountains. The majority of firefighters in China are enlisted as part of the military police and serve two-year fixed-term contracts, so this is as much a barracks and home away from home as a fire station. Inside, a pure-white, cathedral-like space is set aside for ceremonies honoring the bravery of firefighters: a soaring balconied atrium, is, intentionally, not overlit to highlight key architectural features, and therefore provides a harmonious balance of light and shadow. Because of the morphology of the site, the station's plan is quite complex; the building's functions are spread over different levels connected by external walkways. Thanks to the mild climate, these feature various outdoor relaxation areas, reading spaces, and sports equipment, to encourage interaction between off-duty firefighters. Additionally, there are badminton and tennis courts to keep them in peak phyiscal condition.

Coca-Cola Italia Pavilion | **Peia Associates**
| **Milan, Italy**
| **2015**

The Coca-Cola Pavilion, which was built for the Milan Expo in 2015, is an exercise in architectural space and brand experience. The theme for the Expo, which centered on the topic of food, asked participants to consider and question global sustainability while, at the same time, creating a unique, iconic, spatial environment. Little could be more iconic than the Coca-Cola Company's red logo, and 2015 represented its 100th anniversary year. In line with the brief, the architects deployed a series of material choices that resonated with the color—red glass, a rust-orange Cor-Ten steel, and wood—while also reflecting the famous contoured shape of Coca-Cola bottles. The entrance and exit of the building were defined by cascading water,

drawing the natural flow of air in and thereby negating the need for artificial ventilation. Covered in plants and greenery, which contrasted sharply with the iconic red, the structure was designed to suit Milan's temperate climate. For this reason, the building required very little maintenance, and the plants minimal irrigation. In this way, the space sought to reconcile the message of a company with the symbolism of its unique, world-famous product.

Nestlé Chocolate Factory | **Metro**
São Paulo, Brazil
2011

Just off a highway connecting São Paulo to Rio de Janeiro, there is a Nestlé plant where you can learn about the origins of chocolate and see it being made. This eye-catching structure, in Nestlé's brand color red, turns a plain factory visit into a whole "curated tour into the narrative of chocolate production," according to São Paulo architects Metro. The attraction consists of a series of distinctive external walkways that integrate with the existing factory buildings. The Nestlé factory dates back to the 1960s, but was not practically equipped to deal with large visitor numbers or to tell the story of Nestlé's chocolate enterprise in a compelling way; hence, the need for a new approach. Entering the experience via the stair tower, visitors now join a footbridge leading them across the highway, where they join a series of elevated walkways in the factory to view the chocolate production. The walkway structure is made from red tubular steel, which supports the external envelope of triangular glass and expanded steel panels, repeating every 33 feet (10 meters). This makes the structure more rigid, and also has the added advantage of creating myriad reflections of the surrounding landscape.

Red House | **Mildred Howard and Winder Gibson Architects**
Tacoma, Washington, USA
2002

Winder Gibson have a strong track record in creating public art. This small glass house, on display at Tacoma Museum of Glass, was a collaboration with artist, activist, and teacher Mildred Howard, part of the installation _Blackbird in a Red Sky_ (AKA _Fall of the Blood House_). A sharecropper's shack has been rendered in exquisite, deep-red glass. Sharecropping was practiced widely from the 1870s in the American South by former slaves—families rented land from a farmer, giving a share of crops back as payment. Contracts were often exploitative and families ended up in debt. Red symbolizes life, growth, and abundance, but also blood—the shack is a symbol of bloodshed. The structure is simple, made of overlapping strips of glass, clipped together. A cross-rigged wooden frame keeps it stable, and the roof is tilted upward. A meditation on history, home, and the fragility of life, the shack invites us inside to view the cityscape turned red. On an outdoor terrace, next to a glass-like, rimless pool, the house creates exquisite reflections.

Red Shift I: Impregnation | **Cildo Meireles**
London, England, UK
2008

Few spatial artists are as bold as Cildo Meireles. As part of a show exhibited at London's Tate Modern in 2008, _Red Shift I_—an immersive, disorienting "all-red world"—presented visitors with an uneasy sense of a mono-tonal domestic scene. At once familiar and very strange indeed, everything in _Impregnation_ was a bright shade of red—from the clothes in the wardrobe and the cushions on the sofa, to the fruit in the fruit bowl and the food in the refrigerator. Some interpret Meireles' work as referencing human scale in space. When we're faced by a single color expression, in all of the intensity it suggests, there is little we can do but feel. Some might experience an all-encompassing queasiness, while others might feel enlivened

and emboldened. The title of the sequence that this work is a part of—_Red Shift_—connects to cosmic understanding. According to Tate Modern, it references the light that travels to Earth from distant galaxies being stretched "because the space that it passes through is expanding."

In Infinity (from *Dots Obsession*) | **Yayoi Kusama**
Humlebæk, Denmark
2016

Representing the world-renowned artist's first retrospective show in Scandinavia at Louisiana Museum of Modern Art, *In Infinity* spoke a language that embodied Kusama's lifelong obsessions with architectural space, infinity, psychology, and the cosmos. *Dots Obsession*, a field of large-scale inflatable objects in a mirrored room, lent credence to the almost universal and enduring fascination we have with color and shape. White polka-dots foregrounded a bright-red background, forging a dazzling experience in which color was the dominant tool of distortion. Repeating shapes are a staple of Kusama's *oeuvre*. They stem from the recurrent hallucinations the artist has experienced from childhood. She described *In Infinity* as a worldly representation of her own inner landscapes, taking conceptual rooms and making them visceral. What was remarkable about this installation was the way in which it dissolved preconceived boundaries between visitors' bodies and the enclosed world around them—"disappearing into an all-embracing emptiness." While a work of art, this project teaches us that space and color, when deployed well, can provide us with an opportunity to dramatically reassess our built environment, and our position in it.

Leviathan | **Anish Kapoor**
Paris, France
2011

A series of gigantic, interconnecting rubber orbs filling the glass nave of Paris's Grand Palais, *Leviathan* was the fourth annual Monumenta commission. A structure within a structure, *Leviathan* was a massive 37,674 square feet (3,500 square meters) and 115 feet (35 meters) high. On the outside, it was colored like an overripe plum or bruise; on the inside, penetrated by light flooding through the form's glass carapace, its hue shifted to an intense blood red. Allusions to the human body were intentional. Visitors travelled like tiny blood cells around the cavernous, organic spaces, perhaps experiencing a sense of awe as they walked. Red features hugely in Kapoor's work. It is a bridal color in his native India; it is the color of life and death. But more than that, he says: "This overt color, this open and visually beckoning color, also associates itself with a dark interior world. And that's the real reason I'm interested in it." With *Leviathan*, Kapoor created just such a world, with new meanings and mythologies beyond words. It was a work at the heart of the artist's enterprise: "To manage, through strictly physical means, to offer a completely new emotional and philosophical experience."

"Red, red, red, red
When you hear the sound of warning
When the only color is
Red sky in the morning
Everywhere I'm seeing
Red, red, red, red."

Killing Joke | **Band (1978–present)**

May Wind | **Huang Zen**
Qingdao, China
1997

May Fourth Square in Qingdao, Shandong Province, was built in 1997 between the city's burgeoning commercial district and Fushan Bay. It's a popular recreational spot with a green lawn, musical fountain, and this red monument resembling a gigantic spinning top. One of the largest steel sculptures in China, *May Wind* is 98 feet (30 meters) high and 88 feet (27 meters) in diameter; a stack of differently sized red circles wrapping around a central column. Huang Zhen, its designer, is an artist, scholar, and scientist, and has created other urban sculptures in Suzhou, Chaohu, and Zoushan. In 1919, the Treaty of Versailles was drawn up following World War I, under which Germany was subject to various punitive restrictions. Article 156 of the treaty stated that Germany's concession in Shandong, including Qingdao, should be given to Japan rather than returned to China; the Chinese government approved this. Apart from the dent to national pride for the Chinese, Shandong was the birthplace of Confucius, the Chinese philosopher, and the move provoked outrage among student groups who demonstrated in Beijing on 4 May 1919, leading to the creation of the nationalist May Fourth Movement. Eventually, the government agreed not to sign the treaty. It was the start of a shift towards a more populist groundswell in China; anti-feudal and anti-imperialist with the attendant loosening of power by the intellectual elite. Commemorating the dynamism of that movement, the red sculpture celebrates the wind of change.

Per Speculum | **Nicholas Kirk Architects**
London, England, UK
2012

In some cases, the intensity of a color can be heightened by using it sparingly and intelligently. Per Speculum, a temporary folly designed for the London Festival of Architecture in 2012, was one such example: a small-scale passageway built of cheap, simple materials, appeared from some perspectives to be entirely black—and from others to be intensely red. Designed, in the words of its architect, to "force perspective and subtly distort space, scale, and proportion," the structure condensed space in order to accentuate an experience. With a black-and-red checkered artificial turf-like floor, the folly channeled visitors into an intensely dark space, within which surfaces were lined with red. As the light shone through, the colors entered into visual dialog to create a unique experience. At one end of the structure, a small view framed an industrial complex—a surprising intervention designed to reshape the context of the room, and allow visitors to see the environment in an entirely new way.

Harpa Concert Hall | **Henning Larsen Architects**
Reykjavik, Iceland
2011

Harpa is a concert hall and conference venue in the heart of Reykjavik, overlooking the sea and mountains. The exterior of the 301,389-square-foot (28,000-square-meter) building is impressive: the facade, referencing Iceland's spectacular basalt rock formations, consists of hundreds of twelve-sided glass "quasi-bricks," interspersed with colored and mirrored glass hexagonal cells. The "quasi-bricks" are filled with LED units, which light up and change color at night in response to the movement of people inside and outside the building, in an ever-shifting pattern. This was a collaboration between Danish-Icelandic artist Olafur Eliasson and Henning Larsen Architects. Inside, there are four concert halls, an administration area, rehearsal space, and retail area. The main auditorium—the heart of the building—is named Eldborg, after a volcanic crater. This part of the building is the architect Henning Larsen's design; a concrete core inside the glass shell. Eldborg, meaning "fire mountain," is the red-hot powerhouse to the facade's crystalline exterior. The concrete, a material itself suggestive of cooling lava, is surfaced in red-lacquered birchwood, native to Iceland. The auditorium can accommodate up to 1,800 people, with its brutal, shoebox form creating a dramatic contrast to the more prosaic foyer. It has been described as having "a clarity of acoustic that has reportedly moved performers to tears of joy."

The Tiny Travelling Theatre | **Aberrant Architecture**
London, England, UK
2012

This quirky mobile theater was inspired by the home music concerts of Thomas Britton, a seventeenth-century London coal (charcoal) merchant. Britton ran weekly soirées at his home for thirty-six years, popular with high society and the very best musicians of the day, which led to him converting a tiny coal shed at his house on Clerkenwell Green into a performance space, cramming it with musical instruments, including a harpsichord and miniature organ, which was once apparently played by the composer George Frideric Handel. Aberrant Architecture's homage to Britton, the Tiny Travelling Theatre, moved around Clerkenwell during its 2012 Design Week. Able to accommodate audiences of up to six people at a time, the theater, not unlike a miniature organ on wheels, staged plays and storytelling shows, and was towed from place to place by a VW camper van. With boxy projections serving as stalls, it featured a cluster of coal scuttles on the roof funnelling light into the tiny space and referencing Britton's profession. The architects aim was to "revive and explore the intense emotion of a micro live performance." The same year, the little theater ended up travelling as far as São Paulo, Brazil, to the Architecture Biennial.

Càu Thê Húc Bridge | **Nguyen van Sieu**
Hanoi, Vietnam
1865; rebuilt 1952

At the northern end of Hoan Kiem Lake, Càu Thê Húc (or Morning Sunlight Bridge) arches out over the water, connecting downtown Hanoi with a small islet, the site of the Ngoc Son Temple. The Buddhist shrine was built in 1841 to commemorate General Trang Hung Dao's victory against the Mongols in the thirteenth century; it is also dedicated to La To, patron saint of physicians, and to a scholar, Van Xhong. In 1865 the poet Nguyen Van Sieu successfully campaigned for the shrine's restoration. At the same time, he had a new bridge built across the lake—the Càu Thê Húc bridge. Nguyen's bridge in 1865 was a simple wooden-plank affair. Almost a century later in 1952—during Tét, the Vietnamese Lunar New Year—the bridge collapsed under the weight of people making their way to and from the shrine. It was promptly rebuilt by the mayor, Hoang Tin, with support from the French government. The vermilion bridge, arching with sublime elegance from the shore to the islet with fifteen spans and thirty-two pillars, is a well-loved landmark in Hanoi, and much photographed. A tortoise was famously the islet's only permanent resident for many years. After its death, it was preserved by a taxidermist and is displayed in a glass case in the temple.

LFA Irish Pavilion | **TAKA, Clancy Moore, and Steve Larkin Architects**
London, England, UK
2015

This scarlet structure was one of four pavilions designed for the London Festival of Architecture in 2015 to showcase new Irish talent. A collaboration between three practices sharing the same office in Dublin, it was located at the northern end of Cubitt Square, a new development near King's Cross Station. It was juxtaposed with a lemon-yellow pavilion created by Belfast architects Hall McKnight, at the square's southern end. Both were designed on the theme of "Work in Progress." The two pavilions acted in opposition to and in dialogue with one another: while the red pavilion was designed to invite movement and exploration, the yellow one was more static, essentially a library of bricks. The red pavilion featured an elevated passageway reached by steps, a colonnade of chunky concrete columns with a dramatically pitched roof, circular openings, and a repeating facade. Its forms encouraged the curious to climb up, look out over the changing urban landscape, to climb down, and circulate under the Classical–style colonnade, contemplating past, present, and future in the continuously evolving cityscape—a work in progress. The structure was built from a timber frame and panels engineered from woodchips, giving it a provisional feel. Comparisons were inevitably made between this and Bernard Tschumi's Red Folies at Parc de la Villette in Paris (page 21).

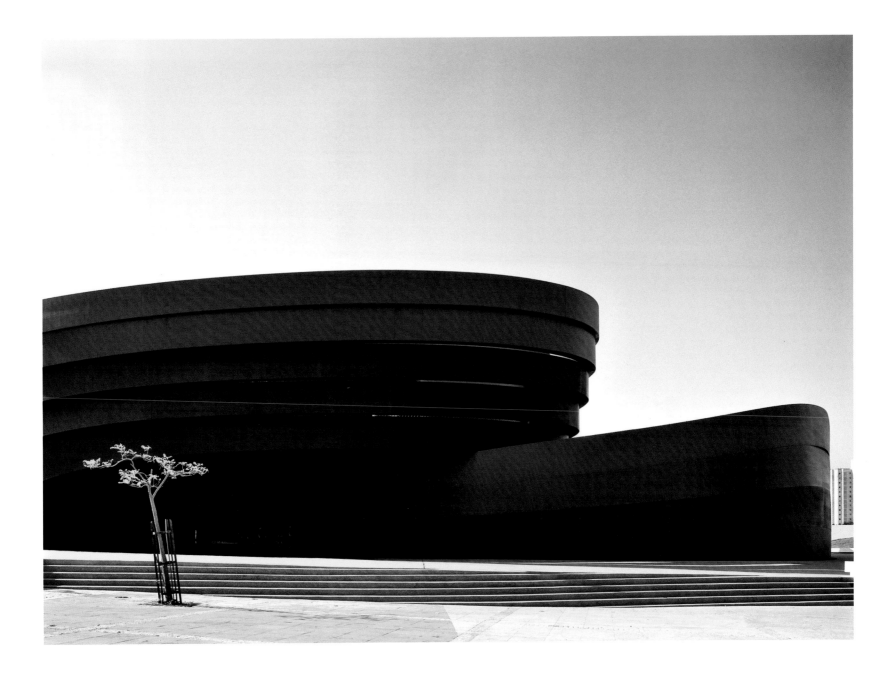

Design Museum Holon | **Ron Arad Architects**
Holon, Israel
2010

The first museum of design in Israel was built as part of a sixteen-year project to develop the city of Holon commercially and culturally, and, fittingly, renowned architect Ron Arad was invited to come up with a spectacular design. It was opened in 2010, which was also the city's seventieth anniversary. Two orthogonal blocks containing white-cube exhibition spaces are supported and contained by a gigantic 300-ton (304-tonne) sculpture of six massive ribbons of Cor-Ten steel. The ribbons flow between the galleries in a figure of eight, enclosing them with long extending "arms," creating sweeping outdoor walkways and gathering spaces for events. Each steel ribbon has a slightly different tone of red from the one adjacent to it—ranging from a deep burgundy to a bright orange—creating an overall striped effect in the sculpture, which recalls the rock formations of the Israeli desert. This was achieved through weathering each steel strip for increasing periods of time—a process accelerated by soaking the steel in hydrochloric acid. Abundant use of wood in the reception area provides a natural juxtaposition with the manufactured steel, adding warmth and tactility. The looping steel ribbons cast fantastic shadow patterns and create a dazzling contrast with the turquoise sky.

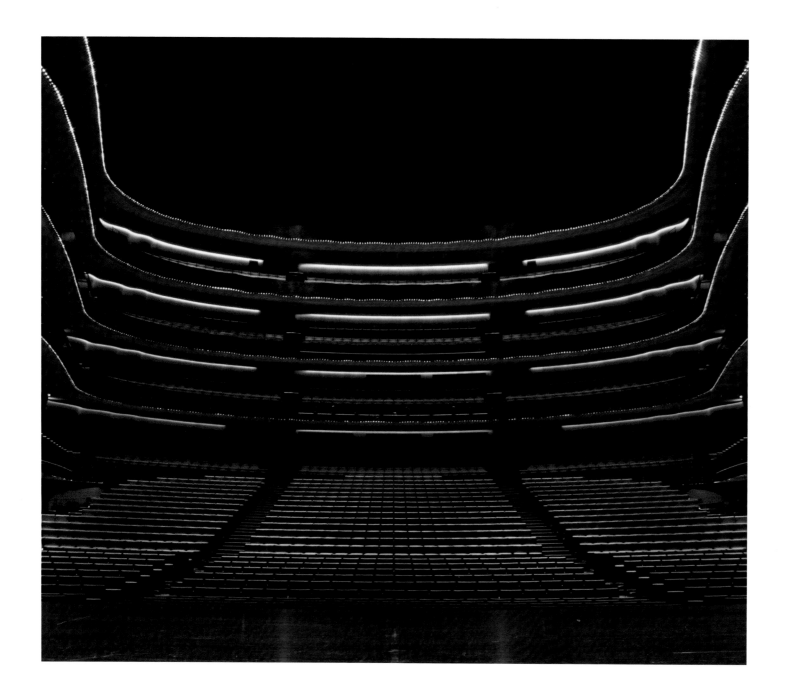

Matsumoto Performing Arts Center | **Toyo Ito and Associates**
Matsumoto, Japan
2004

With one large concert hall and a smaller counterpart, the Performing Arts Center in Matsumoto, Japan, is one of the cultural hubs of the city. On the former site of the city hall, world-renowned architect Toyo Ito conceived a neatly designed series of performance venues occupying a tight inner-city site shaped like a wine bottle. Red is often the go-to color for theaters and performance spaces—it speaks of drama, and is indisputably connected to the almost ubiquitously recognizable velvet-red of the stage curtain. In Matsumoto, Ito has taken this motif to new heights; in one of the performance halls, red seating, lighting, and material finishing forge a complete, unified expression of the color and its symbolism. White is used in ceilings to complement the all-encompassing warmth of the room, which also lends the space a sense of exclusivity and luxury. Any type of performance is a spectacle toward the performer, but also among spectators. This space has a distinct message to send to its patrons: sit back, relax, and enjoy the show.

Formosa 1140 | **LOHA Architects**
Los Angeles, California, USA
2009

Lorcan O'Herlihy's LOHA practice designed this eleven-unit box-like apartment block in a suburban area of West Hollywood. Mindful of creating more green space, both for the inhabitants and the locality, the architects decided against common typologies used for housing blocks: apartments grouped around a central quadrangle, small individual private gardens, or minimal shared spaces between units—all compromises that seemed to miss the mark. By shifting all the accommodation to one side of the plot, they used the remaining space to create a small park, which all apartments would overlook and have access to. This park was also open to other residents of the area. Unsurprisingly the opportunity to create a public garden in LA's

relentless grid was welcomed and incentivized by the city's authorities. Clad in corrugated metal in two tones of red and black, the facade has a slightly utilitarian look. Access walkways face the park, and provide natural ventilation through the building. Perforated metal screening gives privacy to balconies and walkways, and the arrangement of cladding and screening makes for a playfully choreographed exterior pattern. The scarlet block is a joyful and surprising contrast with the rest of the neighborhood's bland suburban architecture. Inside, the apartments are painted in regulation architect's white, set off with accents of—unsurprisingly—red.

Serpentine Gallery Pavilion | **Jean Nouvel**
London, England, UK
2010

Designed for the world-renowned Serpentine Pavilion project, in which the gallery gives free-rein to architects who haven't built in the United Kingdom to create the space of their dreams in London's Hyde Park, Jean Nouvel's proposal was a rhapsody in red. Light, drama, and color formed the leitmotifs of this temporary building in a collection of angular surfaces. More an assembly of parts, the structure resonated with Deconstructivism—an architectural movement that spoke of the architect's own experimental style. For some visitors, the color represented iconically British red telephone boxes and London buses. However, the intention was to play with the contrasts of its context: in a haven of green at the heart of the city, the vivid red danced with the natural surroundings in a scintillating exploitation of color theory. (Designing buildings in a largely empty built environment often serves the function of making space for more liberated design choices.) Large retractable awnings created movable shaded spaces that allowed for a café—brimming with bright-red furniture—and other public functions to operate, whatever the weather.

Theater Agora | **UNstudio**
Lelystad, The Netherlands
2007

Theater Agora was a forward-thinking element of a masterplan for Lelystad in the central Netherlands. Creating a spectacular building supported an ambitious strategy of attracting international artists and performers, and audiences from beyond the immediate vicinity. Two auditoria—one seating 753, the other 207—were built with this in mind. The multifaceted design has been described as kaleidoscopic, and features jutting angles and constantly changing shapes and perspectives. However, its external design came partly from the need to position the two theaters as far away from one another within the building as possible, for acoustic reasons. The choice of color both inside and outside the theater is extremely bold: outside, the steel-plate facade is painted a bright golden yellow and orange. Inside, there is a dazzling use of pink, scarlet, cherry, violet, and white on the main staircase. The large auditorium is a vivid crimson. By way of explanation, architect Ben van Berkel of UNstudio believes that color can inspire people, making them want to stay longer in a building and to return again. The auditorium is lined in a series of concave and convex panels, which not only improves the acoustics but also adds visual interest. Two tones of red have been used to give further depth to the visual effect; the result is an on- and off-stage experience for performers and audiences alike.

Miele Light Box | **Gonzalo Mardones V Architects**
| **Santiago, Chile**
| **2011**

Set in a shady grove of trees on a graveled forecourt, this stylish promotional pavilion was created for the kitchen-appliance company Miele in Huechuraba, Santiago. It aimed to reflect the brand values of Miele products. Firstly, through the idea of lightness—one side of it is cantilevered off the ground so it appears to levitate. Secondly, through the corporate color of the company—a bright, vermilion red. The pavilion was designed for one of the biggest architecture, interior design, and landscaping fairs in South America—CasaCor Chile. A box glazed on two sides resting on top of a podium, the lower part of the projecting facades swept upward at an oblique angle to give the impression that the pavilion was floating weightlessly. Two elevations were in the form of a flattened, archetypal house shape—the others were rhomboid. One facade folded inward to provide a veranda-like terrace area. Packed with Miele products—ovens, refrigerators, and other cooking equipment—it was also enhanced with dark, elegant furniture by Orlando Gatica and a vintage motorbike. In the middle of the space, a bright-red extractor hood emerged from the ceiling, "like an Alexander Calder sculpture," said the architects.

Fushimi Inari-Taisha	Anonymous
	Kyoto, Japan
	711

Fushimi Inari-Taisha is one of Kyoto's most breathtaking sights—a complex of five Shinto shrines stretched across the wooded slopes of Inari-san mountain. It's dedicated to Inari Okami, a deity who brings blessings of health, prosperity, safety, good harvest, and worldly success. Since the founding of this shrine in 711, Inari Okami has been worshipped and prayed to here, but some scholars believe that Inari was followed as early as the fifth century. There are around 32,000 Inari shrines in Japan—a third of all Shinto shrines—of which Fushimi Inari-Taisha is the most important. Visitors walk an atmospheric two-and-a-half-mile (four-kilometer) winding trail through the dense woods up the mountain, under thousands of wooden *torii*, or shrine-gates, arranged in colonnades. The *torii* are painted an extraordinary vermilion with paint made from a combination of mercury and red earth—a formula that's been used for hundreds of years as a wood preservative. In the Shinto religion, the color red is an amulet to ward off evil; but at the Inari-Taisha shrine, it represents, in particular, the plentiful harvests that the Inari-Okami provides. The *torii* are decorated with black script denoting the names of the donors who paid for them.

"If one says 'Red'— the name of the color— and there are fifty people listening, it can be expected that there will be fifty reds in their minds. And one can be sure that all these reds will be very different."

Josef Albers | **Artist (1888–1976)**

Vanke Pavilion | **Daniel Libeskind**
Milan, Italy
2015

Milan Expo 2015 was the city's first world fair since 1906, when it hosted the Milan International Exposition. In 2015, over 140 pavilions were commissioned by participating companies and countries. Daniel Libeskind designed the pavilion for Vanke, a Chinese property company. Libeskind's pavilion was an 8,611-square-foot (800-square-meter) spiraling, glistening, structure exploring Expo 2015's theme, "Feeding the Planet, Energy for Life." The pavilion's design plays with three ideas connected to the theme: first, the *shi–tang*, a Chinese eating hall; second, the landscape, where all food and nourishment comes from; and third, the dragon, a Chinese symbol for farming and sustenance. The pavilion twists around a central axis like the gigantic coils of a dragon's tail. Libeskind insisted on creating the irregular design by hand—no computers were used: "It's really a handcrafted dragon," he has said. The cladding consists of 4,000 metallic-glazed tiles, supported by a steel structure so none appear to touch each other, creating depth with shadow and a wonderfully three-dimensional rippling effect. Inside, there was an exhibition delivered via 200 screens mounted on bamboo scaffolding.

Porta Fira Towers | **Toyo Ito AA, Fermín Vázquez (b720 Arquitectos)**
Hospitalet de Llobregat, Spain
2010

Wedged between El Prat airport and the Catalonian capital, Barcelona, Hospitalet de Llobregat has always been something of a poor relation. These two towers, designed by Toyo Ito—famous for his organic forms—and Spanish practice b720, are part of a masterplan to transform Hospitalet into a financial center and trade-fair zone. Both towers are 360 feet (110 meters) high; one is an office block, the other is a hotel. Together they are a slicker, more modern spin on the fake Venetian towers of the Montjuic Exhibition Center, built to stage the Barcelona International Exhibition of 1929. On plan a simple trefoil plant shape, Hotel Porta Fira twists on its axis as it rises, opening outwards like a flower. Windows are placed irregularly in staccato

rhythm; the crimson aluminum-tube cladding clings at an oblique angle. Twisting, slanting, there is a queasy dynamism about the facade. The blood-red tubing continues inside the hotel as a decorative motif. The office block, with its conventional glass curtain walls, seems like the hotel's much less interesting sibling. But its clever arrangement of sunscreens and a red, elongated X shape, forming the building's nucleus, give the illusion, in certain lights, that two arcs have been gouged from its center.

The Muddus Block | **Wingårdhs Architectural Office**
Stockholm, Sweden
2016

This glistening, lipstick-red housing complex was commissioned by the Stockholm Cooperative Housing Association (SKB), who wanted a new 100-tenant block in the Djurgåden area of the city. Wingårdhs Architectural Office were commissioned and faced a challenge: a directive from the city authorities forbade the use of brick in that area to avoid any competition with, or detraction from, Ferdinand Boberg's Gaslockan—two enormous gasholders built in 1893, and well-loved city landmarks. The architects wanted a red building, but to do this using the same materials throughout meant it had to be in brick. This brick, though, was different from the kind used in Boberg's gasholders: it was outrageous, eye-catching, and bold. The architects

designed a U-shaped, seven-storey block, with a further seven-storey tower nestled in the "U." Almost every component was brick: window and door surrounds, ventilation grilles, and windowsills. Bricks were made to order in Denmark, then shipped to Sweden for glazing in a color the architects later named "Chanel No. 2." A finalist in the Stockholm Building of the Year Competition in 2016, the complex has locally become known—unimaginatively perhaps—as "the red building."

Keiun Building | **Aisaka Architects**
Tokyo, Japan
2014

On one of the key routes to the Yoyogi National Stadium, Aisaka Architects have created a unique facade to give shape to an otherwise orthodox building. The four-storey structure, which accommodates retail spaces on the ground floor and office spaces above, features a woven surface facing the street in a palette of reds, browns, and many hues in-between. Aluminum sheets are knitted together, referencing a brick building that once occupied the site. This woven surface has a practical function—sun-shading. From below, the facade appears to constrict and, from some angles, the sheets look like corrugated metal. They have, however, been assigned random positions, as opposed to being set in a calculated formation; their relationship to one another is more a result of designers' intuition than anything else, a move that ensures if one ribbon becomes damaged, it can be easily replaced without disrupting the flow of the rest. In this building, the investment was placed on its outward-facing personality—as a result, it has become one of the more recognizable buildings in this bustling area of Tokyo.

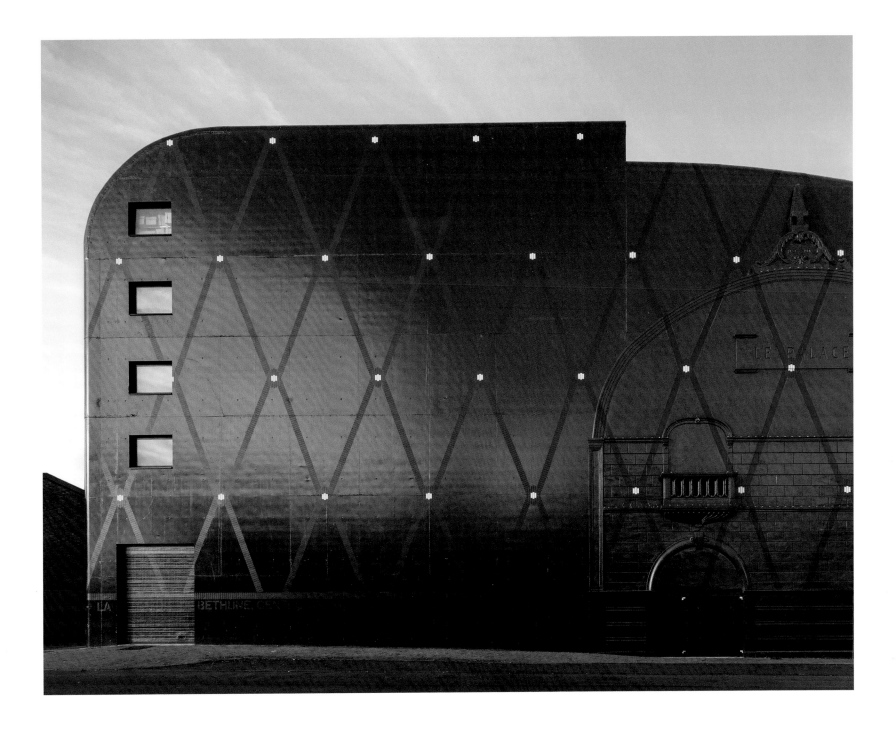

Comédie de Béthune | **Manuelle Gautrand Architecture**
Béthune, France
2014

Comédie de Béthune is one of thirty-four playhouses around France that have been granted national status as part of a postwar initiative to decentralize and democratize French theater. Previously located in an old gunpowder store, in 1999 the city's theater needed to find a new permanent base. Eventually an imaginative location was found—the shell of a former 1930s cinema, Le Palace. Manuelle Gautrand won the competition to convert what was left of the cinema into the theater's new home. A voluminous, softly curved concrete structure was designed, with a facade of dark-burgundy glazed tiles, suggesting the classic red upholstery of old theaters, and decorated with a lozenge pattern. An extension was planned as part of the development, subject to an adjacent building being demolished; this lead to Gautrand working on the theater again, designing the new wing which would house a large rehearsal area. A block shape at right angles to the theater space, the extension reprises the lozenge motif with its exterior of black-metal panels, providing a contrast to the oxblood-red structure.

Blood Center | **FAAB**
Raciborz, Poland
2013

The bright red of its facade leaves no doubt as to the function of this medical center in Raciborz, southern Poland. Designed to encourage people to give blood, the four-storey building includes a donor hall, a center for blood screening and processing, laboratories, administrative offices, conference rooms, a specialized blood bank, plasma repository, and roof terrace. Its most interesting feature is the custom-made glazing on the elevations, in the tradition of the Silesian ceramics of the region, which can be seen in the nearby historic center of Katowice. Three shades of red are used: a vivd, bright red, representing oxygenated blood in the arteries; and two darker shades of red, representing blood in the veins containing carbon dioxide. Smaller tiles are used on the ground floor; the upper levels include ceramic panels and, for the first time in Poland, curved glazed panels. The rounded elements in the architecture such as the corners of the building represent the biological, whereas the straight elements represent the technological. Inside, the glazing continues in the stairwells, and the carpets are blood red.

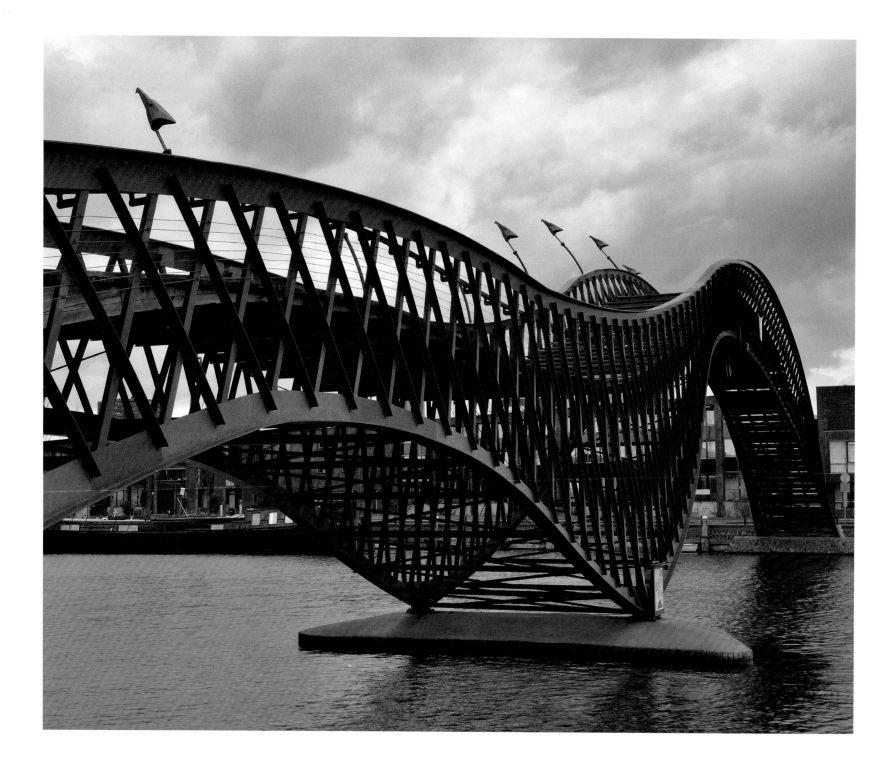

Python Bridge (Hoge Brug) | **West 8**
Amsterdam, The Netherlands
2001

Amsterdam is well known for grand architectural statements—and for urban infrastructure. The *Hoge Brug* (High Bridge)—also known as the Python Bridge—is one of three that spans the canal between two islands, Sporenburg and Borneo. A bright beacon in an otherwise low-rise neighborhood, the bridge marks one of the only pedestrian routes across the water. Its remarkable height serves two functions: allowing pedestrians exceptional views across the water and surrounding islands, and allowing sailing boats to pass and berth in a nearby marina. Its snake-like appearance mimics scaled skin, and lampposts lend it a Jurassic-period air. Painted a striking ruby red that provides a stark contrast with the blue-gray canal waters, and built in 2001, it is also one of the newest of the city's approximately 1,200 bridges. For some it's a snake (as it is known colloquially), for others it looks more like some kind of prehistoric carcass. Both readings attest to its status among its neighbors: whether they love it or loathe it, they can't ignore it.

Han Show Theater | **Stufish Entertainment Architects**
Wuhan, China
2014

The Han Show Theater is part of a masterplan to develop a cultural district for the central Chinese city of Wuhan, capital of Hubei Province. An impressive 230 feet (70 meters) high and 328 feet (100 meters) in diameter, the theater is shaped like a Chinese lantern; bright red, it is unmissable against the Wuhan skyline, and at night it is lit up to create beautiful reflections in the Donghu Lake. The elliptical shapes crisscrossing the facade reference bicycle wheels, another Chinese icon, which are supported by a mesh of 25,000 illuminable bright-red disks. These are inspired by Chinese bi-disks, ancient artefacts dating back to Neolithic times which came to be associated with the circularity of life and ideas of the afterlife, stars, and cosmology. The theater's interior is equally impressive, decorated with gold and white, and can comfortably accommodate an audience of 2,000. The architects, Stufish, specialize in musical, theatrical, and cultural structures, creating stage sets for Madonna, U2, the Rolling Stones and Queen.

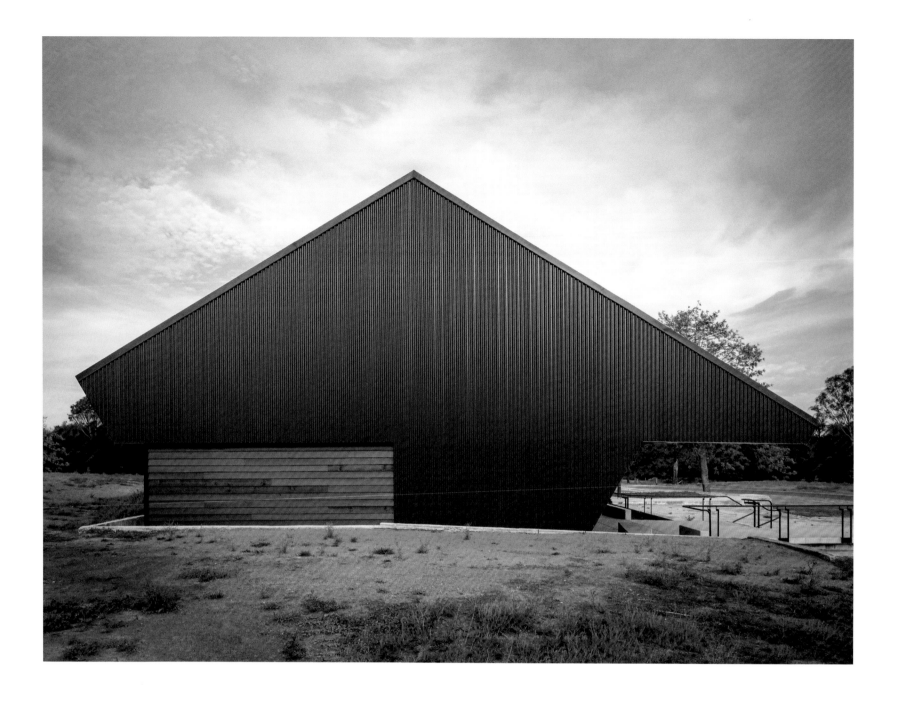

The Condensery | **PHAB Architects**
Toogoolawah, Queensland, Australia
2015

The Condensery occupies a packing shed, built in the 1920s and once part of a sprawling condensed-milk factory. Much of this complex was destroyed by fire in the early 1950s, and it was over five decades before the remaining structure was selected as a central hub for the cultural life of Toogoolawah, a small town in rural Queensland, Australia. Occupied by a gallery and a workshop, much of the building remains untouched. Concrete floors and walls, alongside an exposed iron roof structure, form the core of the space's characteristics—in this way, the architects state, history remains legible. The most striking alteration takes the form of a varied color palette. It is, put simply, a red box in the center of largely empty but continuously green landscape. Within this verdancy, the deep-red hues of the facade declare its position in time: at once old, of a former era, and at the same moment strikingly contemporary. This ambiguity becomes more evident on approach; the clarity of the box diffuses into a set of prominent details, cuts, and material choices. The building stretches out into the landscape by way of terraces occupying the foundations and remnants of former, lost, factory spaces.

National Building Museum | **Montgomery C. Meigs**
Washington, D.C., USA
1887

The National Building Museum in Washington, D.C. aims to educate and inspire people about architecture, engineering, landscape design, and construction. Its magnificent red-brick building, constructed between 1882 and 1887, was commissioned to house the headquarters of the United States Pension Bureau. The Civil War (1861–65) had greatly increased the number of pensions paid out by the federal government; in the 1880s, a staggering one-third of its total budget was reserved for pensions. The building also commemorates those who fought on the Union side during the conflict with a 1,200-foot (366-meter) terracotta mural, and provides a space for functions. Designed by U.S. Army Quartermaster General

Montgomery G. Meigs, it was his last architectural work and the one of which he was most proud. "Meigs's Red Barn" was inspired by two Roman palaces: Palazzo Faranese, for its Classical, orderly facade with alternating pointed and curved window pediments; and the early-sixteenth-century Palazzo della Cancelleria, which was the model for the interior's enormous hall, with its open, arcaded sides. Congress stipulated that brick must be used as it was fireproof, keeping citizens' records safe.

Kiruna Church | **Gustaf Wickman**
Kiruna, Sweden
1912

Kiruna is in the Arctic Circle, the northernmost city in Sweden. Its existence, and location, is due entirely to one of the largest iron-ore deposits in the world. The city was founded in 1900 by the mining company Luossavaara–Kiirunavaara Aktiebolag (LKAB), and then grew at breakneck speed. Kiruna's rust-colored church sits on top of a hill overlooking the mine, surrounded by birch trees. LKAB's founder, Hjalmar Lundbohm, said to the architect Gustaf Wickman, "design a church in the form of a lappkåta," a wooden-plank wigwam built by the indigenous Sami who live in the region—which he duly did. On the roof stand twelve gilded six-feet-six-inch- (two-meter-) high sculptures, made by Swedish sculptor Christian Eriksson and cast in

bronze. They represent different states of being human, including inspiration, reflection, despair, bliss, love, and humility. The city of Kiruna is, however, soon to undergo a massive transformation. The extent of the mining activity in the city is causing ground subsidence and some buildings to crack and collapse. LKAB is paying to reconstruct all of the affected buildings two miles (three kilometers) to the east. That includes this church, which, in 2025, will be painstakingly dismantled, piece by piece, then reassembled in Kiruna's brand-new city center.

Casa Rossa | **Thomas Radszuweit**
Ascona, Switzerland
2007

Framed by mountains, the Casa Rossa (Red House) occupies a stunning position on the shores of Lake Maggiore, Ascona. Reinforced concrete is the main material used for the building, allowing a sense of volume and minimalism. The sleek and elegant home is L-shaped: the house's two wings are arranged around a courtyard with patio and generously sized swimming pool. The red tint of the concrete complements the similar rock tones of the nearby mountains. Casa Rossa is arranged over a single floor, with three bedrooms, a living room, and a dining room; however, its west wing contains another living space, which is part of a double-height tower with mezzanine. The tower gives the house a fortress-like demeanor, and projects an air of stability and solidity. Inside, the home is as minimalist as outside, with white décor designed to offset a contemporary painting and sculpture collection. Red-toned wood is used for decking to complement the concrete and natural stone used for detailing elsewhere around the property.

La Roche Sur Yon Bridge | **Bernard Tschumi & Hugh Dutton**
La Roche Sur Yon, France
2010

In Bernard Tschumi's La Roche Sur Yon Bridge, aesthetic principles merge with function to create a local icon. Above a high-speed train line, the bridge connects the world-renowned pentagonal city of La Roche Sur Yon with more recently developed neighborhoods. Described by the architects as "a symbol of contemporary urban relationships," the core concept of the project is organic structure. In other words, the engineered structure of the bridge takes its form from natural geometry, carried forward in the smallest of details as well as the whole. As people pass over the bridge, they are protected from the weather by interlaced polycarbonate surfaces that diffuse the wind and rain without forming a hermetically sealed barrier against them. For architects, the bridge is about movement, and the experience of wandering through a town or city; hence, it forms a part of the routes that people take rather than being an experiential obstacle. Its bright red-orange coloring turns the bridge into a beacon, as opposed to a muted expression of functionality.

"All my life I've pursued the perfect red. I can never get painters to mix it for me. It's exactly as if I'd said, 'I want Rococo with a spot of Gothic in it and a bit of Buddhist temple'—they have no idea what I'm talking about. About the best red to copy is the color of a child's cap in any Renaissance portrait."

Diana Vreeland | **Fashion Editor (1903–1989)**

House N | **Cheng Franco Architects**
Piura, Peru
2017

In the coastal region of Piura, Peru, House N is a private residence at the heart of an expansive 24-acre (10-hectare) site. Used by its owners as a place to breed the famous Peruvian Horse, the architects were tasked with designing a small family home with large social areas and a room to house equestrian trophies that would by sympathetic to its isolated surroundings. Clad in Cor-Ten steel, the building has a uniquely agricultural atmosphere. Its facade has the character of the earth—a deep, dark, reddish brown. The larger mass of the building is suspended above the ground, allowing spectacular views through the house and across the landscape of open fields and deserts. Circulation up and through the house, which has an altogether lighter material atmosphere, is by way of a spiral staircase and bridges that connect the different rooms of the upper storeys. Inside, windows frame the views and allow the residents to keep an eye on their stables during the day. The trophy room disrupts the smooth, minimal style to create a treasure trove of alcoves—a space, in the words of its architects, to "contemplate."

Pago de Carraovejas Winery | **Amas4arquitectura**
Peñafiel, Spain
2003

In an idyllic location overlooking the Botijas Valley and Peñafiel Castle, this vineyard in Valladolid produces tinto fino, cabernet sauvignon, and merlot. With its hillside location, the winery uses gravity in the winemaking process. The new winery was designed to envelop older, existing structures, and the complex consists of series of a long, low buildings housing a visitor center and offices, and halls for every part of the winemaking process. The visitor center and offices are the most spatially varied volumes of the complex, with cantilevering forms that create areas of shade for offices and recessed terraces giving views over the countryside. The heaviness of the industrial buildings is deliberately balanced with areas of blank space, voids, and patios. A specially formulated red dye was mixed with the concrete to evoke the color of the wine produced there. Board-forming, a process by which concrete is given a patterned, wood-grain effect, provides the plant with a textured and more rustic surface, perhaps a nod to the wood of the barrels that the wine slowly ages in. One thing that is for sure is that the plant's architecture expresses the same attentiveness and quality control that goes into making the wine itself.

Celtic Museum | **Kadawittfeldarchitektur**
Glauburg, Germany
2011

In the rolling hills of Glauberg, on the site of an ancient Celtic fortified settlement near Hesse, Germany, the Celtic Museum is a contemporary intervention in a historically charged site. Positioned close to a burial mound, the building was conceived as a marker in the landscape and, for this reason, stands as a beacon in a place of profound archaeological significance. As a result, it had to appear different. The architects chose to clad the building—which is distinguished by its rigid, structural shape—in Cor-Ten steel, perfectly suited due to its rusted metal, earthy-red finish. In many ways, it feels as though it has itself been excavated. Visible for miles, the building is partially integrated in the hillside. In the words of its architects, it amplifies the burial mound's leading role in the ensemble. A large, panoramic window projects toward the open countryside, providing a place from which visitors can survey—and thereby begin to understand—the scope and prominence of the site. Inside the museum, no route is suggested—rather, visitors are encouraged to discover the landscape and its meaning by wandering and, much as an archaeologist might, giving in to intuition.

Garden of 10,000 Bridges | **West 8**
Xi'an, China
2011

West 8's submission for the International Horticulture Exhibition of 2011 in Xi'an, the Garden of 10,000 Bridges, consisted of labyrinthine paths through a sea of high bamboo, around 16 feet (5 meters) high. The paths looped and crisscrossed, and there were five—rather than 10,000—bright-red humpbacked bridges as crossing points, where visitors could climb high up above the bamboo line. The garden, with its meandering paths, serves as a metaphor for life, with its many twists and turns punctuated by occasional moments of epiphany. To that end, it was only up on the bridges that visitors were able to see where they were: a pause to gain some perspective before re-entering the jungle-ike journey. Up high, they glimpsed those on other bridges,

making a visual and social connection with people on similar paths. In many cultures, the bridge is a metaphor for transition, a place to look forward and back, a liminal space between one state and another—and indeed, West 8's intention was to reflect "the need for creating symbols in the production of landscape." The bridge has also been an important feature in Chinese garden design for millennia, and the country has developed innovative techniques for bridge construction, so it's a fitting motif for this fun social project which brings people and landscape together.

Cibercentro Macarena | **Mediomundo**
Seville, Spain
2010

Cibercentro Macarena, located in Seville, Spain, is a cyber-center, previously the site of a basketball court. From the outside, the building has a simple material expression. Crimson-lacquered metal sheets define it as a focal point in an otherwise gray and subdued environment. The solidity of the facade dissolves at the top to reveal an open roof terrace with sheltered views toward its surroundings, which include a nearby river. Housing computing equipment for public use, the building has an open groundfloor designed to encourage passersby to enter, which also connects to the wider public area. A cafeteria and multipurpose room comprise the main spaces of its interior, which also serve the purpose of what the architects describe as a "WiFi Plaza"—in other words, it's a space for being among others as you connect, communicate, and learn. Windows open toward the street, shielded by bright-red louvers. As a result, the building is always able to maintain its bright, bold identity: a place that encourages meeting and collectivity, even if it's only through the medium of a screen.

Gentle Genius | **GG-loop**
Altamura, Italy
2015

This is a clever and daring refurbishment of a corner house in Altamura, Apulia, southern Italy. It was inspired by a King Crimson album, *In the Court of the Crimson King*, which, according to the architect Giacomo Garziano, had inhabited his subconscious and emerged through the project in a "cathartic" way, allowing him to imagine "a new urban music score." The multifaceted steel facade creates "an ever-moving surface," and the project is designed to rupture the town architecture's existing rhythms, awakening the *genius loci,* or the spirit of a place, once more. The 2,519-square-foot (234-square-meter) facade is clad in crimson steel, fashioned to create geometric patterns with almost endless visual interest. A

753-square-feet (70-square-meter) roof terrace completes the home, which is divided into two apartments. The interior is just as extraordinary, featuring a multi-sensory installation called "The Infection"—a cocoon-like structure seen as an extension of the human body. It is complemented by an ultra-modern furniture range designed by Garziano. Gentle Genius won him the Young Italian Architect Award of 2016 and is part of the "house-museum" project The Seed of Time; it was used for a performance by the artists' collective Elephants & Volcanoes in 2015. The house has been listed on Airbnb, where you can "be part of your own performance," hosted by Garzanio's parents. Proceeds go toward funding cultural events.

LAP Marina Residence | **5+1AA Alfonso Femia Gianluca Peluffo**
Milan, Italy
2014

The LAP Marina Residence in Milan, Italy, is a compound of luxury modern residences with the atmosphere of a medina. Milan is the most rapidly growing city in northern Italy, and has been a site for contemporary architectural experimentation since the dawn of the twenty-first century. In many ways though, this project signifies a different ambition: in the words of its architects, to reinvent "local and continental roots" by "reinterpreting African identity." Streets weave their way through the estate by way of a grid, all enclosed by vibrant red-ocher walls. The volume and height of the buildings, which embody certain Mediterranean vernaculars and northern African architectural styles, reinforce a sense of modern elegance in a fast-paced world. In creating self-enclosed and protected properties—the brief from their client—the architects sought to also build in a sense of permeability between the residences, manifesting as a careful balance between what is deemed private and what is deemed public. The project represents an intelligent solution to handling the challenges of modern-day life, deploying color to heighten a sense of community and connect the individual homes to form a cohesive whole.

The Couch | **MVRDV**
Amsterdam, The Netherlands
2015

IJburg, to the east of Amsterdam, is a part of the city where 18,000 new homes, across ten artificial islands, are being built to solve the capital's housing crisis. IJburg Tennis Club, open 365 days a year and completely free, is one of the many amenities designed to attract people to the area. The club needed a pavilion and grandstand overlooking their center court and the rest of the sports ground. However, there was not enough space to have both without encroaching on the all-important courts area. The innovative solution that MVRDV came up with was The Couch: both clubhouse and spectator platform in one building. The roof of the pavilion dips elegantly to create a quirky and informal seating area for 200 people. The long, rectangular club building has panoramic views of center court, and on the other side, overlooks IJ Lake, with its landscaped greenery. Inside, the ceiling swoops down dramatically to create a cozy, nook-like space. Clad in FSC-certified wood, it's a warm, bright, and homely space, with colored seating and a log-burner for colder days, plus a café. The clubhouse has been sprayed with an EPDM polymer the same color and texture as the terracotta-colored clay court to ensure a good match between the two areas.

Monument to Pedro Almodóvar | **Sergio Garcia–Gasco**
Calzada de Calatrava, Spain
2009

The film director Pedro Almodóvar is celebrated by this imposing monument in his hometown, Calzada de Calatrava, in La Mancha. In a park on a small hill, the monument resembles the proscenium arch (the frame separating the stage from the auditorium) of a theater—Almodóvar often uses stage or film sets within his films as a dramatic device—or an Art Deco cinema screen. Its form also acknowledges the concertina body of an old-fashioned camera. More than a grandiose folly, the monument is also functional, a venue for outdoor cinema screenings and open-air performances, and it's the location for the Almodóvar Award ceremony that the town hosts annually. The flat, endless La Mancha landscape captured within the structure is like a frame from one of Almodóvar's films. The director's cinematography has a bright, Pop art aesthetic, and red is the director's favourite color, denoting intense emotion and drama. The monument's red concrete pays homage to this: dry and self-compacting, it was mixed to exact color specifications at the factory and hydrated only once on site to ensure tonal uniformity. It is decorated with a molded, circular 1960s-style pattern, which again suggests Almodóvar's set designs. But, interestingly, the motif also resembles eyes or conjoined pairs of spectacles—referencing the act of looking, and the wondrous spectacle of his exuberant, outrageous films.

Espace Culturel de La Hague | **Périphériques Architectes, Marin + Trotti Architects**
Beaumont-Hague, France
2015

This extraordinary sight is located near a bland housing estate on the Cotentin Peninsula in Normandy. A stunning new arts center for Beaumont-Hague, it was a bold commission by the local council, and its statement architecture is designed to sing against the flat, gray Normandy landscape; a pulsating fusion of polished surfaces and convulsed red steel that insists on drawing you inside. The center is a compact two-storey block from which two L-shaped areas have been subtracted, creating an interplay of volume and void. A multi-faceted structure made from perforated vermilion steel panels gouges its way through the core of the building, rearing up through the void at the rear and re-emerging at the front. The snake-like shell twists through a double-height atrium, creating a visceral, sculptural tunnel which, as well as adding drama, has sound-muffling qualities. On either side of the atrium there are two wings: one for a school of performing arts, with music, theater, and dance studios; the other for the auditorium and community rooms. Polished concrete, wood, and raw steel are used widely inside. The center's facades are glazed curtain walls giving tantalizing glimpses of the creative activity within, and act like gigantic mirrors that reflect stunning visual panoramas of cloud and sky.

Bridging Teahouse | **Fernando Romero Enterprise**
Jinhua, China
2006

This is a bridge that is also a space in which to wander, meditate, or just absorb the views of green landscape beyond. Mexican architect Fernando Romero was commissioned to design a pavilion at the Jinhua Architecture Park, a venture dreamed up by artist Ai Weiwei to commemorate his father, the poet Ai Qing. One of seventeen structures dotted along the Yiwu River, the pavilions are designed by architects from all over the world, including Herzog and de Meuron, who masterplanned Jindong New District where the park is located. The park has been described as a reinterpretation of a traditional Chinese garden. Within this context, Romero's design brings together two traditional Chinese garden forms: the bridge and the teahouse.

2,691 square feet (250 square meters) in area, the roughly N-shaped concrete structure spans a pond. The bridge has a honeycomb-like facade, partly glazed, with trapezoidal and triangular openings which provide "captured views" at every juncture. Inside, it consists of a series of "micro-levels" connected by zigzagging flights of steps. There are a variety of spaces—with some smaller and more intimate, so people can escape the crowds of visitors that pass through. The striking red coloring symbolizes happiness and prosperity, but, disappointingly for some, no cups of tea are served there: it's a metaphorical structure.

Staircase III | **Do Ho Suh**
London, England, UK
2011

A staircase made of translucent red nylon was Do Ho Suh's enigmatic creation for the Istanbul Architecture Biennale in 2003. This was the first of a series of installations he has made based on 1:1 scale—copies of real staircases in places of importance to him, such as his apartment. For the first Istanbul version, a thread staircase ascended to a fabric canopy held up by pillars, creating a fragile second level. This version of the staircase, *III*, was created by Do Ho Suh in 2011, displayed at Tate Modern, London—this time inspired by his Chelsea apartment in New York. Giving the staircase such a dissonant color as red, was, apparently, a conscious way of removing it from its normal context, intensifying the dream-like effect of seeing it hovering above our heads. He's particularly preoccupied with the memory of architectural spaces, and with structures that imply a transition or crossing-over point—staircases, bridges, or doors. He was born in Korea but has lived in the U.S. and London, and he describes such structures as metaphors for his sense of cultural displacement. Architecture, for him, is a primary way of mediating his own existence: "I experience life moving through a different series of spaces."

Austin | **Smart Design Studio**
| **Surry Hills, New South Wales, Australia**
| **2013**

A former timber warehouse and workshop for lathe-manufacturing has evolved into this smart, wedge-shaped crimson block in Sydney's eastern suburb of Surry Hills. Once a working-class quarter that was home to the rag trade and other light industry, the area is now gentrified and popular with Sydney's younger and wealthier inhabitants. The basement and ground-floor levels of the mixed-use complex have been transformed into a commercial space with retail units; above these are two floors of high-end apartments. The warehouse's roof was lifted to create a penthouse with fantastic views over Surry Hills with a balcony spanning the entire length and side of the building, overhung by a cantilevering roof to allow a generous outdoor space. Because of the building's wedge-shape, all the apartments vary in dimensions and layout. Enormous new rectangular openings—spanning two floors—have been integrated within the concrete beam-and-column facade. They have hand-painted steel frames in rust red to compliment the "Hot Chili" render, a color close to the original hue of the building. With a nod to its industrial past, the old Brackenbury Austin signage—the name of the company that used to own the building—was retained. Now it's known more minimally, and elegantly, as Austin.

"Even if you don't like colors, you will end up having something red. For everyone who doesn't like color, red is a symbol of a lot of culture. It has a signification, but never a bad one."

Christian Louboutin | **Fashion Designer (1964–)**

Maison Bernard | **Antti Lovag/Studio Odile Decq (restoration)**
Théoule-sur-Mer, France
2015

Antti Lovag's Maison Bernard in Cannes slides down the Massif de l'Esterel like a gigantic creeping mat of tapioca. It's a prime example of the Hungarian architect's philosophy of "habitology"—a loose concept that included banning right angles and straight lines. Circles and curves, he thought, were closer to nature and closer, too, to the human body. Arriving in France in the late 1940s, Lovag worked with Jean Prouvé and later Jacques Couëlle, one of the first French architects to develop an organic style. In close collaboration with automobile magnate Pierre Bernard, his client, the two developed Bernard's family home gradually, completing it in the late 1970s. Lovag first got to know the terrain, creating an iron frame without foundations, that was then covered with mesh, concrete, and two layers of fiberglass-reinforced polyester. After Bernard's death, his children Isabelle and Jean-Patrice wanted to preserve this extraordinary house. Odile Decq, commissioned to renovate it, spent five years on the project. Most of the craftspeople who worked on the house had worked on the original building with Antti Lovag. Decq had a similar working relationship with Isabelle Bernard as her father had with Lovag; renovating the house slowly, in stages. The interior was fully restored and rooms were decorated in pink, purple, and orange, with one room being a synthesis of all the house's colors. The Maison Bernard Endowment Fund now supports the project and is open by appointment.

Gmurzynska Gallery | **Roger Diener**
Cologne, Germany
1991

Located in a high-end residential district in the south of Cologne, the Gmurzynska Gallery comprises two connected cubes; one large, one small. Set back from the street and positioned in a lightly wooded area, the building is clad in cedar—some as vertical panels, others as large rectangular boards—and colored a soft, deep red. Built on a burnt-red brick plinth, this combination of materials finds a "muted echo," in the words of the architects, against its subdued suburban context. Visitors ascend a set of red brick stairs to enter the build-ing—a surface material that blends into a unified ground condition. Once inside, the rooms of the gallery are bright white and flooded with southerly light from above—from the outside it's unclear, initially, how and where this light enters. At the rear of the building, a sculp-ture terrace extends into a garden and operates as an extension of the exhibition spaces. Filled with cherry trees that bloom a muted pink in spring, this garden embodies the vitality of the changing light and seasons—a gesture expressed throughout the project, which balances simplicity and precision in equal measure.

Red Square | **Archiworkshop**
Bucheon, South Korea
2016

This refreshingly avant-garde take on the suburban home uses red brick to create a sense of pure abstraction. From the street, it appears as a windowless brick square. But this is actually the side of the building, concealing a cleverly designed, three-storey home for three generations of one family in Bucheon, Seoul. The L-shaped structure exists as two separate but interconnecting dwellings—the ground floor allocated to the grandparents, and the young family on the upper two levels. The ground-level apartment includes a master bedroom, kitchen, living room, laundry room, toilet, and access to the garden. The second apartment's living room and bedrooms are on the first floor, while the library and recreational space is on the top floor, opening out onto a roof terrace. A staircase between the two connects the families, allowing them to remain separate, but together. The sides of the house facing away from the street are a clean, bright white, but the street-facing facades are windowless blank canvases, clad entirely in brick, punctuated only by doorways. They create a sense of introversion for the house but also arouse curiosity, making it distinct from the other "regulation" suburban homes in the area. The red, monochrome brick facade references Dansaekhwa, a style of minimalist, abstract Korean painting that uses muted, earthy colors and came to prominence in the mid-1970s.

Casa das Histórias Paula Rego | **Eduardo Souto de Moura**
Cascais, Portugal
2009

The great silos of Casa das Histórias—vaguely industrial but rustic, church-like, but secular—are an unmistakable symbol of this museum dedicated to Portugal's most celebrated artist, Paula Rego. Located in the smart coastal town of Cascais, a short train ride from Lisbon, the gallery opened in 2009. Rego herself commissioned Eduardo Souto de Moura to design the space. It houses a permanent collection that spans fifty years of her career, a small display of work by her husband, Victor Willing, and 8,073 square feet (750 square meters) of exhibition space in total. The museum's pyramidal forms are reminiscent of another famous Portuguese building—the medieval National Palace in Sintra, with its pair of great chimneys. The work of Raul Lino, who designed buildings in Sintra; much of Cascais; and its neighboring resort, Estoril, could also have influenced de Moura: Lino liked to add pyramidal turrets to his elegant, wistful villas. The other striking feature of the museum is its material—a terracotta-red concrete which, in the huge cuboid forms of this building, starts to resemble the clay-like material used in Portuguese farmhouses. Apart from its two unmistakable towers, the museum is a one-storey, four-winged building arranged around a central room housing the main collection.

La Maison Rouge | **Amédé Regis Mulin**
Mopti, Mali
2007

This soft-red, fifteen-room mansion was designed as a hotel by French architect Amédé Regis Mulin. A contemporary Banco construction using sun-dried mud, chaff, and water, it was completed in 2007 and fuses European and African architectural styles. 17,760 square feet (1,650 square meters) in floor area, the three- and four-storey arrangement of two buildings around a tree-filled courtyard is located near the Bani river in Mopti. Due to the military coup in Mali, and ongoing political crisis that followed, the hotel closed in 2012. Banco masonry is an extremely skilled craft, taking years to learn: apprentices are appointed to a master who teaches them everything. This house is a wonderful example of how traditional building methods

can be used in a modern context with stunning results. The plasticity of the mud, shaped by hand and trowel, has allowed for some extraordinarily beautiful detailing. The magnificent terrace gives the hotel a sense of grandeur, openness, and space, but there are also many shady nooks for sitting, with circular and arch-shaped openings for light and ventilation. Walls in the public areas and bedrooms are smooth but include detailing—such as small triangular, square, or arched niches for displaying ornaments. Red floor tiles, or tomettes, designed by Mulin and different in every room, were hand-made by Mopti potters.

Rivera Estudio	**Juan O'Gorman**
	Mexico City, Mexico
	1932

Once home to Frida Kahlo and Diego Rivera, the Rivera Estudio in Mexico City is part house, part artist's studio, and part photographic laboratory. Its architect, Juan O'Gorman, worked in the vein of Modernist Le Corbusier and the Dutch School of architecture—an approach defined by functionalism and, in the case of the latter, using primary colors as signifiers of space. Reinforced concrete is the building's language, its surfaces in many cases left untreated. Given its function, natural light was of paramount importance in the design; especially so in the studios. An external spiral staircase connects the three storeys that comprise them, emerging from and returning back into the crimson wall. This color, set against tableaux of white, recalls

Mexican heritage and building techniques, connecting this Modernist project with the deep roots of its context. The colors deployed function as a bridge through time; this building makes a declaration about the cross-pollination of architectural styles in a way that is at once sympathetic, and was indeed remarkably daring for its time.

Oasia Hotel Downtown | **WOHA**
Singapore
2016

Sometimes only an icon will do. The Oasia Hotel in Singapore is one such example: a soaring skyscraper, clad in shades of red aluminum mesh ranging from crimson to rose, and punctuated by a vertical forest. Positioned in the heart of the city's business district, the project represents a prototype for how greenery might be deployed in structures at the heart of a densely packed, land-scarce urban center in a tropical climate. Its architects chose to design a series of sky gardens, in layers, making the most of its highly overlooked position. This is a building not only preoccupied by what happens inside, but also what happens on the outside: how it is viewed by its neighbors and passersby, and what it might be able to give to the wider city.

Each sky garden is considered a separate veranda, with open views and a sense of climatic permeability. Here, the breeze passes through, allowing public spaces to remain comfortable and shaded even in the warmest weather. Its facade is, in a sense, landscaped. Designed to provide a haven for local wildlife—birds and animals alike—creepers, vines, and shrubbery ornament it. A tropical bower, or shaded area, crowns the vivid red tower, making the most of every available space, and encouraging biodiversity in an otherwise intensely man-made environment.

International Accommodation Center for the Oceanological Observatory

Stéphane Fernandez, Atelier Fernandez & Serres
Banyuls-sur-Mer, France
2013

Banyuls-sur-Mer, on the French Mediterranean coast, is home to an important oceanological observatory: the Arago Laboratory, part of the Université Pierre et Marie Curie. This accommodation block was built in 2013 for the many visiting researchers and students who come from all over Europe to study the unique flora and fauna of the nearby Cerbère-Banyuls marine nature reserve. The monolithic structure is in a prominent place on the seafront, making explicit its purpose and connection with the sea, and cuts a striking sight from across the marina, vividly contrasting with the town's orange rooftops. Its red ocher color is inspired, say the architects, by the color of the soil of the nearby hills, rich in iron oxide. But the other more obvious comparison is with the color of coral, and coral's form is suggested by the intricate and beautiful concrete screen enveloping the entire building. During the design process, an algorithm was used to distribute the different frond-like shapes in a dynamic and naturalistic pattern. Behind this screening, the bedrooms are accessed by external corridors also serving as social spaces and balconies. As well as providing privacy, the screens have a cooling effect during the fierce Mediterannean summers.

Free Trade Wharf | **Holder Mathias Alcock**
London, England, UK
1987

It's as if two Italian hill towns have been beamed down to Tower Hamlets. At Free Trade Wharf, an enormous jumbled arrangement of dwellings cascades down to the River Thames, rising to form two peaks. This staggering development of 208 flats stands on the Thames's north bank, on a dockland site owned by the historic East India Company. It adjoins two warehouses built between 1795 and 1796 that have been converted into apartments—a deliberate fusion of new and old. The red brick of the development respects the tone of the older warehouses and looks especially effective in such a voluminous mass against the river and sky. The site was bought in 1977 by the Inner London Authority with the intention of building a campus for London Polytechnic (now the University of Westminster), but it never materialized. The land was acquired by Regalian Homes, and the first Free Trade Wharf flat was sold in 1987. The development consists of one-, two-, or three-bedroom dwellings, and unusually—perhaps a selling point in the individualistic 1980s—no two apartments have the same internal layout. Terraces and balconies give huge views of the River Thames. The complex has a gym, sauna, and swimming pool and extensive landscaped gardens—something uncommon for London, where space is at such a premium.

Embassy of the Netherlands | **Bjarne Mastenbroek and Dick Van Gameren**
Addis Ababa, Ethiopia
2005

Built on a sloping plot in a grove of eucalyptus trees on the outskirts of Addis Ababa, the architects' priority for this embassy was to create a complex of buildings that blended in with its natural landscape. Red-hued concrete, the color of the Ethiopian earth, is the main material used. The development includes the chancellery, accommodation for diplomatic staff, the ambassador's house, and even a small school, but so subtle is its presence, it looks as if it has always been there. The use of board-formed concrete and the massive, geometric forms—particularly the huge cantilever at the entrance to the chancellery—give the whole complex a Brutalist sensibility. Concrete was the only locally available choice as a construction material; however, wood and stone were also integrated into the ensemble. It really does look as though it has been carved out of the landscape, like the monolithic, rock-hewn churches in the Ethiopian town of Lalibela. But gentle detailing, such as the rounded corners of windows, give a sense of refined elegance. Finally, in a nod to the watery Dutch landscape, there is a shallow pond on the roof of the chancellery.

CINiBA | **HS99**
Katowice, Poland
2011

CINiBA is a scientific-information center and academic library, part of the University of Katowice, Poland. Red sandstone is used to create a grid of panels on every side of the center, and makes a visual connection with nearby existing brick buildings, but on an exaggerated scale. The panels are arranged in a staggered formation with slot-like openings between each. At night, golden light shines through the slots, transforming the building into a glowing powerhouse of energy and activity. The library houses a range of scientific and economic collections for the University of Silesia, most of which is centered around a three-storey atrium. This hall is dominated by a ribbon-like, concrete stairway; pre-cast concrete panels on the interior walls and widespread use of pale wood on the other staircases and flooring give the space a stripped-back, utilitarian feel—an acknowledgement of the industrial heritage of Katowice. The exterior red panels are visible through the building's glazing, adding a warm orange tone to the interior palette. The grid motif used outside on the brick facade is repeated often inside, in the flooring and internal glazing—suggesting the orderly management of information via the activities of research, science, and learning.

Der neue Zollhof | **Frank Gehry**
Düsseldorf, Germany
1998

Der neue Zollhof is part of Düsseldorf-Hafen, the redeveloped port area of the city. The complex is situated at the eastern edge of the harbor, an area also known as Medienhafen, a reference to the many media and fashion companies based there. The landmark commercial development, with far-reaching views up and down the Rhine River, consists of three separate buildings. Built in the Deconstructivist style that Gehry is well known for, the complex features curving and angular volumes and window frames projecting from the facades. It represents a radical shift for German urban architecture, which is frequently restricted by tough planning laws. The east tower is clad in white plaster, the middle one in stainless-steel panels, and the west tower, pictured here, in red brick. This eleven-storey structure differs in more ways than one from the other two—it is formed of a series of geometric towers, leaning and huddling together. The unifying element of all three buildings, however, is the window openings, which are identical on all three. The German newspaper *Die Zeit* described der neue Zollhof as *schunkelnd*—which translates as "swaying"—the significance being that it describes the rhythmic movement people make when listening to traditional German beer-drinking songs.

Entrance to the Tomb of I'timād-ud-Daulah | **Anonymous Agra, India 1622–28**

Sometimes known as Agra's "baby Taj," the Tomb of I'timād-ud-Daulah is an exquisite monument predating the Taj Mahal by four years. It was built as an act of love by a grieving daughter. I'timād-ud-Daulah was the name given to Mirza Ghiyas Beg, a Persian noble who arrived at the Mughal Court and swiftly worked his way to the top of the government hierarchy during the reign of Akbar I, the third Mughal emperor. Jahangir succeeded Akbar in 1605 and gave Ghiyas Beg the title, meaning "pillar of the empire." His daughter eventually married Jahangir in 1611, and she was renamed Nur Jahan, meaning "light of the world". Known for being exceptionally artistic, she was independently rich through trading and land ownership, and a major patron of architecture. On her father's death, she inherited his wealth and thus commissioned this tomb for her parents in Agra. The complex is designed in typical Indo-Islamic style; the courtyard is entered via two of four sumptous portal gates—two are decorative rather than functional, for the sake of balance. Faced in red sandstone, it has geometric and *chini-khana* designs inlaid into the stone with white marble. These are carved decorative recesses: in this case some are real and some false—and appear to contain vessels, bowls of fruit, or flowers. These are symbols particularly associated with Jahangir's reign.

"Any red is rooted in blood, glass, wine, hunters' caps, and a thousand other concrete phenomena. Otherwise we would have no feeling toward red and its relations ..."

Robert Motherwell | **Painter (1915–1991)**

Lucky Knot | **NEXT Architects**
Changsha Meixi Lake District, China
2013

NEXT have a track record of designing interesting bridges: they were behind the arched metal Melkweg Bridge in Purmerend, the Netherlands, in 2012. With offices in both Amsterdam and Beijing, the practice was ideally placed to design an astonishing walkway over the Dragon King Harbor River in China the following year. 607 feet (185 meters) long and 78 feet (24 meters) high, the bright-red bridge is in the rapidly developing city of Meixi Lake, a new, state-of-the-art ecological area covering 1,675 acres (678 hectares) to the west of Changsha. The bridge's steel spine curves in a graceful, infinite loop. It is actually three separate bridges, connecting points at different levels across the river (the river banks, road, and the park, which is at a higher level.) It also has connecting points across the three bridges, which pedestrians access by walking through "moon gates"—circular portals traditionally used in Chinese garden design. The connecting points also add stability to the structure. The bridge's final form is ultimately a result of knotting all these elements together, creating a beautiful lattice of gently curving waves of steel. In Chinese folk art, the knot represents luck and prosperity, and so it was seen as a fitting symbol to adopt for a thriving new cityscape. At night, the bridge plays host to a spectacular LED lighting show.

Center for Interpretation of the Battle of Atoleiros | **Gonçalo Byrne**
Fronteira, Portugal
2012

The Battle of Atoleiros, in Alentejo, Portugal, was fought on 6 April 1384, between the kingdoms of Portugal and Castile. Portugal had no crowned king and was in the grip of civil war. The Castilian attack on Fronteira was defeated despite the Portuguese being outnumbered (5,000 Castilians to 1,400 Portuguese.) Heavy losses were suffered by the Castilians, while the Portuguese, using a defensive square formation to brilliant effect, apparently suffered none at all. Seen as a defining moment of Portugal's resistance against Castile, the episode is still important to contemporary national identity and was marked by the creation of this museum in Fronteira in 2012. The museum is located in the town center, overlooking an urban park which represents the battleground in this square configuration. A low, rectangular building running alongside the park, the museum is split into a series of narrative display rooms showing works by artist Martins Barata and opening up perspectives of the represented battlefield. Its roughly textured, tinted red concrete evokes the color of the Alentejo earth, and of course, the bloodshed. The journey around the building comes to a close in a contemplation space overlooking the metaphorical battlefield. The reception is adjacent to the exhibition block, with the two elements separated by a void. Viewed from the side, it looks like the smaller entity is standing up to the much larger one.

Kunshan Visitor Center | **Vector Architects**
| **Jiangsu, China**
| **2014**

This luxury hotel at Yangcheng Lake in Jiangu Province, China, is built on an idyllic 200-acre (81-hectare) organic farm. Guests can pick their own seasonal herbs, fruits, and vegetables, later prepared for them at the hotel—or on the farm under a lakeside tent. Up to 80 lbs (36 kg) of honey a day is produced in the farm's beehives. Guests can choose to join chefs for cooking demonstrations in one of two glass pavilions—one overlooking rice fields; the other, a lily pond. The farm also has a visitor center that consists of a small complex of buildings incorporating a reception, multipurpose space, and kennels arranged off a central external corridor. The architects' main priority was, on this rural site, to ensure that the buildings had a minimal visual impact on the environment. As such, they're low-key and subtle interventions; two of the buildings, when viewed from the farm, appear as totally screened. One is veiled in perforated burnt-sienna Cor-Ten steel; the other is hidden by red wooden louvers running the length of the building. These screens protect the interiors from the low evening sun and allow cool breezes to penetrate the buildings. The rear of the center is clad in more rusted steel, arranged in a chequerboard pattern, which casts abstract shadows in the evenings. The overall effect is of natural serenity in an abundant, fruitful landscape.

Red Fort | **Anonymous**
| **Delhi, India**
| **1648**

This spectacular fort clad in red sandstone was the main residence of the Mughal emperors for 200 years until 1856. Shah Jahan, fifth Mughal emperor of India, moved the capital from Agra to Delhi, naming the new city Shahjahanabad; the fort was constructed at the same time and was named "Qla-a-Mubārak'a," "the auspicious citadel." Begun in 1639 and completed in 1648, this was the first Mughal fort based on a geometric grid pattern within a roughly octagonal form. Pavilion structures are set within the grid, and are connected by a water channel called the Stream of Paradise. At its peak, it accommodated 3,000 people, and the complex incorporated a Hall of Public Audiences, royal baths, a Palace of Color, and a white marble Hall

of Private Audiences. The centerpiece of this was the magnificent Peacock Throne, with jeweled and enameled gold birds on its canopy. The fort was planned according to Islamic style, but the pavilions show decoration from the Hindu, Timurid, and Persian traditions. It was the first Mughal palace to incorporate *jali*—marble screens pierced to form lattices. Unfortunately, Shah Jahan never got to live in his palace: his son Aurangzeb put him under house arrest at Agra Fort for the years leading up to his death in 1666.

Songzhuang Art Museum | **DnA**
Beijing, China
2006

Songzhuang, just under an hour from Beijing, has become something of a creative enclave for the capital—a staggering 5,000 artists were living in the district by 2015. This bunker-like contemporary-art museum was built to engage with and display the work of its burgeoning community of creatives. The gallery complex consists of four cube structures, differing in height in a staggered arrangement, resting on top of a wide, glazed podium base. The concrete structure is clad in a startling Titian-red brick. The ground floor features a massive exhibition area lit from either side by the panoramic glazing and an awe-inspiring, double-storey, hangar-like hall with skylights, big enough to display the most monumental art. Everywhere

you look, huge vistas of utilitarian white space open up to let the main event—the art—sing. The only real ornamentation in this ocean of blankness are the staircases, with sculptural filigree sides. The upper floor holds yet more exhibition space, but it's introverted, enclosed, and windowless, with daylight streaming in from above. A massive 53,820 square feet (5,000 square meters), this is a gallery that's justifiably confident it will attract leading artists and impressive visitor numbers.

Hotel Danieli | **Anonymous**
Venice, Italy
1400s

Overlooking the waterfront avenue of Riva degli Schiavoni, Hotel Danieli is archetypal Venetian Gothic in style. The facade of the red-pink hotel, formerly Palazzo Dandolo, has marble sills, and balconies with Gothic arches featuring typically ornate traceries. The roof is topped with obelisk-shaped chimneys. The palace's most outstanding feature, though, is a beautiful, four-storeyed courtyard with an elegant, colonnaded staircase. The courtyard floor is paved with gleaming terrazzo Veneziano—a mixture of stucco and marble pieces unique to the city. The hotel actually consists of three interconnecting palaces. Palazzo Dandolo is the oldest, built at the end of the fourteenth century by the noble and powerful Dandolo family. In the early sixteenth century, the palazzo was split into three apartments and used for lavish social events. In 1824, a Mr Giuseppe Dal Niel (also known as Danieli), a hotelier from Friuli, rented out the whole of the second floor of the palazzo, turning it into a hotel. Nearly a year and a half later, seizing an extraordinary commercial opportunity, he bought the whole building. Now a luxury hotel with 210 rooms, it was enlarged to include the nineteenth-century Palazzo Casa Nuova, previously the city's treasury, and the Palazzo Danieli Excelsior, built in the twentieth century. Famous guests have included Goethe, Wagner, Proust, and Balzac.

IULM Milano | **5+1AA Alfonso Femia/Gianluca Peluffo**
Milan, Italy
2014

The International University of Languages and Media in Milan was founded in 1968; its campus is located in the southwestern part of Milan. This striking tower is part of a composition of three buildings designed for the university by 5+1AA; the complex also includes a low-rise, emerald-green-domed auditorium with underground car park, and a two-storey analogue library to its north. The russet-colored tower is home to IULM's archives and digital library. On three sides of the tower, the windows are minimal, consisting of small square openings positioned in irregular rhythm—reminiscent of the holes punched in tickertape, one of the very earliest forms of digital communication. Lower light levels in an archive are a positive benefit,

even when it is digital, keeping computers and servers from overheating and making on-screen reading easier. To ensure some illumination, however, the north-facing facade is made of pyramidal glass bricks, allowing soft light to infuse the archive. Pale-blue portholes punctuate the terracotta concrete facades, and bright-red external staircases snake from one floor to another—but their random placing suggests an aesthetic rather than primarily functional value.

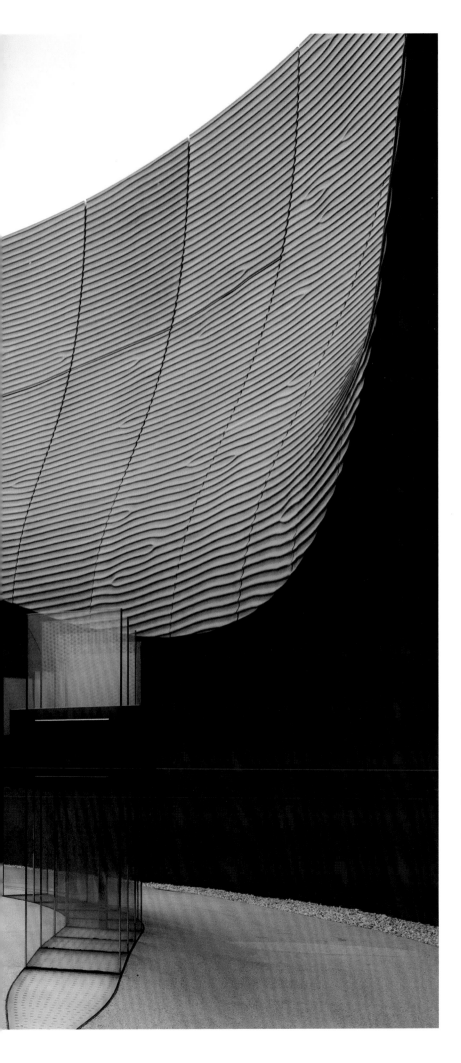

UAE Pavilion, Milan Expo | **Foster + Partners**
Milan, Italy
2015

Foster + Partners have been involved in major development projects for the United Arab Emirates in recent years, including the master-planning of Masdar City in Abu Dhabi, a brand-new, carbon-neutral, zero-waste model metropolis, ready for a post-oil future. The practice was therefore a natural choice to design the UAE pavilion in 2010 at the Shanghai Expo, and again in 2015 in Milan. The 2015 pavilion, seen here, was based on the planning and layout of the country's traditional desert cities. Occupying a large site close to the heart of the Expo, visitors accessed the pavilion from the main walkway through the fair and entered a canyon-like "street" with 39 foot (12 meter) sides, referencing the high walls and self-shading, narrow streets of a desert settlement. Throughout the site, the undulating Glassfiber Reinforced Concrete (GRC) walls featured an elegantly ridged pattern based on the scan of a sand dune. As they walked through the orange-red corridor, visitors could look at digital monitors in copper-clad cases with information about the UAE. They then continued up a ramp to a drum-shaped auditorium where they watched a state-of-the-art presentation enhanced with augmented reality. The pavilion won the Expo's best exterior design award that year.

Second World War Museum | **Studio Architektoniczne Kwadrat**
Gdansk, Poland
2017

Bursting dramatically from the ground at an angle of 56 degrees, this red-brick building suggests rupture, a metaphor for the way that war shatters the world's everyday realities. The Museum of the Second World War in Gdansk is divided into three spaces, representing the flow of time: the underground floors, with exhibitions representing the past; the space surrounding the museum, the present; and the structure rearing from the earth, with viewing platform, denotes the future. Located not far from the Motlawa River, the museum has far-reaching views over the city. But the space epitomizes conflict in more ways than one, particularly in terms of the narratives it proposes. Opened in March 2017, the museum had been a joint initiative between national government, led at the time by Donald Tusk, and the local government of Gdansk. Its aim was to present a broad view of the 1939–45 conflict, particularly within the context of Eastern Europe—and also from the perspective of civilians, featuring many donated artefacts from ordinary people. The conservative government, however, led by the PiS party, criticised this approach as being too universalistic and "not Polish enough." A court hearing has now ruled that the museum must merge with another, smaller, and as yet unbuilt museum in Gdansk, the Westerplatte, which focuses more specifically on the Nazi invasion of Poland.

Stralsund Town Hall | **Anonymous**
Stralsund, Germany
c. 1250

The town of Stralsund in northeast Germany has been designated a World Heritage City for its outstanding medieval architecture. With a unique island location, situated between three lakes and the Strela Sound along with its sister town, Wismar, Stralsund was a strategically important member of the Hanseatic League—the commercial and political federation of the Baltic and North Sea in the Late Middle Ages. Because of this affiliation, there was a constant exchange of ideas, technical knowledge, and culture between the member towns. Consequently, Stralsund enjoyed great wealth, and constructed several impressive "Brick Gothic" buildings—the town has three monumental churches in this style, and the town hall is a further outstanding and well-preserved example. Brick was the favored building material in the region, owing to the lack of stone. Clay, however, available from the northern German plains, was in plentiful supply. Brick Gothic was influenced by Italian Gothic architecture, but the northern-European style was bulkier and more monumental. The Stralsund town hall is a prime example of secular architecture adopting this idiom. The complex was built as a four-winged traders' hall, with small shops and stalls on both sides of its inner courtyard. Work on the "show facade" begun around 1310 and continued to be refined until 1350. A baroque, two-storeyed colonnade was added to the courtyard in the seventeenth century.

Yves Saint Laurent Museum | **Studio KO**
| **Marrakech, Morocco**
| **2017**

This museum, in the heart of Marrakech, is a short distance from Jardin Majorelle—the Moroccan home owned by Yves Saint Laurent and Pierre Bergé from 1980 to Saint Laurent's death in 2008. The museum's exhibition spaces combine with a research library and archives to create a dynamic, expressive testament to the high-fashion designer's life and *oeuvre*. A two-tiered facade, which symbolizes the weft and warp of interwoven fabric in two shades of red, reflects, in turn, the climate and the landscape of its context: deserts and dunes, sharp shadows, and the bright North African sun. Its architects, who were informed by the archives of Saint Laurent, observed the designer's creative tendency toward curved lines running against straight. Elegant and understated but defiant and bold, the structure iterates these tropes. The building is a succession of contrasting themes—delicate and fearless, with an almost lacey material expression. At its center, a circular courtyard captures the sunlight at its zenith to retain its warmth. Inside, the representation of the red heat of day gives way to the more mellow tones of wood and stone.

Hawa Mahal | **Lal Chand Ustad**
Jaipur, India
1799

This stunningly ornate palace in Jaipur had one function: to keep noblewomen hidden from the public. It was built as an extension of the nearby Royal City Palace, and is also known as the Palace of the Winds. Maharaja Sawai Pratap Singh, the ruler of Jaipur between 1778 and 1803 and member of the Kachwaha Rajput caste, ordered the architect Lal Chand Ustad to design it. Women in the royal household were under strict orders to remain in purdah: the Hawa Mahal would allow them to watch processions and festivals without breaking this rule. The scholarly Pratap Singh also found the palace an inspiring spot for his poetry-writing. Hawa Mahal is a blend of Hindu Rajput and Islamic Mughal architecture. Built in red and pink sandstone, in the pyramidal form of Lord Krishna's *mukut*—his headdress or crown—its elaborate facade is punctuated by 953 honeycomb-latticed windows allowing cool breezes, blowing from the west, to enter the palace. The intention was for each woman of the royal entourage to have her own window. The shallow, five-storey structure is little more than a facade, and the street-facing side is actually the back; the front of the building is extremely plain. Pratap Singh was clearly pleased with the building, because Lal Chand Ustad was given a *jagir* for his work—a district of land and all the revenues that came from it.

"A good painter needs only three colors: black, white, and red."

Titian | **Painter (1488–1576)**

| *The Impossible Staircase* | **NEXT Architects**
Carnisselande, The Netherlands
2013 |

At the top of a grassy hill in Barendrecht, south Rotterdam, there's a playful sculptural staircase inspired by the form of a Möbius strip. Named after the German mathematician August Ferdinand Möbius, his famous strip is a surface with only one side and only one boundary. Barendrecht is an area split in two: Carnisselande is a new suburban development to the west of the A29 motorway; "Old" Barendrecht is to the east. In planning Carnisselande, the council set up a cultural strategy for the area, commissioning twenty-five public artworks in a scheme called *The Elastic Perspective*. These imaginative follies included a giant concave mirror; an arrangement of metal sheep on a playground carousel; and this design, also known as *The Impossible Staircase*. Although from a distance the staircase resembles a Möbius strip—the pathway twists around onto the sculpture's underside—it's a clever illusion and it's impossible to follow the staircase all around its surface. More practically, the staircase can give people an elevated, uninterrupted view of the city skyline. The folly surely also references Dutch artist M.C. Escher, who designed his own famous infinite staircases. Made of weathered Cor-Ten steel, its bright orangey red contrasts brilliantly with the green, grassy landscape.

Vlooyberg Tower | **Close to Bone**
Tielt-Winge, Belgium
2014

A giant steel staircase to nowhere rises above Kabouterbos Forest in Tielt-Winge, Belgium. The 36-foot (11-meter) structure replaced a wooden lookout tower on the same spot that had been burned down. The local council wanted a replacement, but it had to be absolutely vandal-proof, include a shelter, and be at least 30 feet (10 meters) high. Engineering studio Close to Bone's extraordinary response to this brief was a playful and seemingly gravity-defying staircase. The visibility of the north-facing tower was important. It was designed specifically to be easy to spot from the N2 Leuven-Dienst main road and become a local landmark. The cantilevering staircase comprises several galvanized-steel sections clad in weathered Cor-Ten steel. Its color is a reference to the red-brown ironstone found in the region—a rock from which iron can be smelted commercially. The tower has two dampers to prevent the staircase from shaking as people climb up it; all engineering calculations were done by hand. At the top, there is an enclosed viewing platform where visitors can look over the surrounding countryside through small peepholes. Winning a national award for steel construction in 2014, the project was described as "a stairway to heaven." The surreal folly was assembled in just half a day.

Červenà Lhota Castle | **Anonymous**
| **Jindřichův Hradec, Czech Republic**
| **Mid-1500s**

This fairytale red castle, rising up from its own rocky island, is north-west of Jindřichův Hradec in South Bohemia. The first fortress on this site was built in the mid-fourteenth century, in Gothic style on a granite outcrop, which, after a stream was dammed, became an island. Between 1542 and 1452, the castle was rebuilt in Renaissance style after it passed to the knightly family of Káb of Rybňan, when it was renamed Nová Lhota. *Nová* means "new;" *Lhota* means "due period," and is the name for a medieval settlement where residents are excused from paying taxes for a time in return for farming the owner's arable land. The castle has four wings around a courtyard, with crow-stepped gables and turrets. In 1597, Vilém Růt

of Dírná had the castle rendered with red plaster, naming it Červenà Lhota (*červenà* means "red"). Gruesome local folklore says that a devil-possessed woman died horribly there, her blood staining the pure-white facade, and that it was colored red in memory of this tragic event. No-one knows if this is factually correct, but perhaps Růt also knew it would look stunning next to the green woods surrounding it, and magical reflected in the lake. Červenà Lhota was requisitioned by the Slovak government in 1945, and became a children's hospital; the following year, it was declared a national cultural monument and opened to the public in 1949. The castle can only be reached by a stone bridge, which replaced the original drawbridge.

Caring Wood | **James Macdonald Wright & Niall Maxwell with Rural Office for Architecture**
Kent, England, UK
2016

In the county of Kent, England, Caring Wood is a contemporary interpretation of a country house. Built in a verdant agricultural landscape, it's striking in form and color: angular, truncated trapezoid, and pyramidal volumes reference the oast house, a hyper-local vernacular used for kilning hops in preparation for brewing. Clad in orange-red, terracotta-toned clay tiles and coppiced chestnut cladding, the house is built almost exclusively from locally sourced materials. It accommodates an extended family who would like to live together, and at times apart, under the same roof. Inside, the warm hues of the exterior dissolve into pure white walls and wood detailing. Beneath one of the cone towers is a secluded courtyard

and reflecting pool, designed as a private space to relax in while making the most of natural daylight. This is a project which exudes a certain domestic warmth, while neatly connecting to the canon of the great English stately home. In this way, it is a sensitive weaving and reinterpretation of national and local ways of building—a testament to the landscape in which it sits.

Quinta da Tilia | **Pedro Mauricio Borges**
Ponta Delgada, Portugal
2015

In the Portuguese Azores, Quinta da Tilia is a low-lying home close to the sea and surrounded by verdant green gardens. Simple in form, the house is authentic in construction; it expresses its external shape and volume internally in the same way as it does externally. Arranged linearly, the building extends its reach across a lush, cultivated landscape defined by a stone wall that orchestrates the site to, in the words of its architects, "embrace the tree's shadow circle." Rendered light red, the exterior of the house bends to hug the landscape near and far. The green of its surroundings is also integral to its internal atmosphere. Transparency—in the form of large windows and skylights—seeks to dematerialize the body of the building in order to bring the light, shadows, and colors of the trees inside. A tin roof, which defines the red hue of the complex, belies its wooden structure. From within, however, this becomes evident: all of locally sourced Cryptomeria wood, Quinta da Tilia is finely attuned to the location of which it is a part.

Turbenthal Forestry Center | **Burkhalter Sumi Architekten**
Turbenthal, Switzerland
1994

One third of Switzerland is covered by forest, and the country has the biggest wood reserves in Europe. In the early 1990s, Christian Sumi and Marianne Burkhalter were commissioned by Zurich's city council to design a prototype for forestry-operation centers that could be rolled out in four locations. The architects devised a modular approach, allowing centers to be configured according to the terrain and foresters' varying needs. There were three parts to the "kit:" an office area with storage lockers; a garage for cars and forestry vehicles; and a spacious, sheltered, open-sided barn for storing timber and other forestry materials. With the exception of the garage—which had to be made of reinforced concrete because

of fire regulations—the principal material for the huts was, appropriately, wood. The barn was stained scarlet, a contemporary spin on the brown-red wood stain used on rustic Swiss buildings. The garage and barn form one unit; adjoining this in staggered formation is a long, rectangular office structure on stilts. Both building elements are parallel to the hillside. The office's roof pitches sharply to drain water, and its form echoes the hilly terrain.

Nebuta-no-ie Warasse | **Molo, d/dt, Frank La Riviere Architects**
| **Aomori, Japan**
| **2010**

Every August, the city of Aomori in northern Japan hosts an extraordinary event attracting three million visitors. The Nebuta Matsuri Festival sees giant, illuminated paper sculptures of heroes, demons, and animals from Japanese myths and stories carried on floats through the streets to a deafening cacophony of bamboo flutes and *taiko* drums. The Nebuta floats are amazing sculptural pieces, created from scratch for each festival, full of dynamic realism, humor, and color. A museum to tell the story of the Nebuta Festival and to house a collection of the floats was opened in 2010. Strategically located next to Aomori railway station, overlooking the sea at Aomori Bay, the box-like rectangular structure is enclosed by a shell of rust-red,

39-foot- (12-meter-) tall steel ribbons, creating an external walkway. At various points, the ribbons are bent and folded to make doorways and windows. Inside the commanding space, visitors can learn about the history of the Nebuta before heading up to a hall with polished black-concrete floors, black stucco walls, and a black ceiling where the floats glow in darkness. The hall is connected to another space via huge sliding doors, so the heroes, demons, and animals can be brought alive through performance.

La Muralla Roja | **Ricardo Bofill**
Calpe, Spain
1973

Throughout his career, Ricardo Bofill has wholeheartedly embraced color. In the Costa Blanca resort of Calpe, his sprawling, high-walled La Muralla Roja (The Red Wall) is the antithesis of the bland, white holiday block. Towering above the clifftops, resembling a fantastical citadel, it has obvious Moorish influences: the high walls of a Moroccan kasbah, castellations, and courtyards. In addition, Bofill exploits the plasticity of concrete to create abstract patterns of interlocking vertical and horizontal planes. The fifty apartments cluster in modules in the rough form of a Greek cross; much of the development is painted a delicious, soft, earthy red, but other tones—pinks and blues—have been used intelligently to create dazzling visual effects

in the intense Spanish light. The complex often features in fashion shoots, color blogs, and music videos. La Muralla Roja is part of Bofill's larger Manzanera development, which took nearly two decades to complete. It includes two other blocks, El Anfiteatro and Xanadu, and has sports facilities, a restaurant, bar, and swimming pool. The fortress-like Xanadu is as astonishing as its red neighbor. Bottle green, it stands in glorious counterpoint to La Muralla Roja, mimicking the form of the nearby Peñon de Ifach crag.

Bardill Studio | **Valerio Olgiati**
| **Scharans, Switzerland**
| **2007**

This soft, earthy-red concrete shed is an exquisite, bespoke studio designed for a storyteller and musician in Scharans, a village in western Switzerland. Valerio Olgiati was commissioned to create a space for the artist on a site where a barn once stood. Planning permission was only granted on condition that the new building would be of exactly the same volume as the old barn. The result is a strangely otherworldly structure—rural but industrial. The artist, Linard Bardill, only needed one room to create in—this occupies less than a third of the space that was available. The rest is taken up by a monumental courtyard space with an enormous circular roof opening, so the artist can work on ideas with views of sky and clouds overhead. The

dark-red concrete used looks like clay—suggestive of the creative process, of shaping and molding. It has a tactile quality that's enhanced by the embossing of a floral motif on the walls, inside and out. This could be a simplified mandala form or a Swiss meadow flower, but it adds organic decoration to the austere expanses of concrete. Bardill lives within walking distance of the studio, but this is more than a private workshop for one artistic individual—it is also open to the public once a week and hosts events, becoming a more extroverted space that also adds to the cultural life of the local community.

CRICOTEKA Museum of Tadeusz Kantor | **Wizja Architects & nsMoonStudio**
Nadwiślańska, Poland
2014

The CRICOTEKA museum in Nadwiślańska, Kraków, is a volumetrically bold building on the banks of the Vistula River. From a distance, two shapes come into view: a historically charged, two-storey structure and a second, vast, building that wraps round and over it. This second structure represents the contemporary addition, and relates to the existing structure through the mirror-clad underside of the new building. In this way, the roof of the historic building is reflected, and thereby visible to people passing alongside the water. The second structure is clad in Cor-Ten steel, giving a matted-bronze, red-brown effect. This is a building defined by the materials it exhibits; an unconventional example of how two very different structures can exist as one in symbiotic tension. In spite of its perceived heaviness, it is also playful: as a center for art, it is itself unrecognizable as either gallery or museum. In other words, it provides space for creative use without predefining what that might mean. In the words of its architects, the "purpose of creative activity is not in identifying the structure as a form, but rather in the way it interacts with its environment."

Geometric Hot Springs | **Germàn del Sol**
Los Rios, Chile
2005

In Chile's southern lake district, an extraordinary, red, zigzagging boardwalk drops down through a rocky gorge past a series of geothermally heated bathing pools. The water of the Aihué stream, fed by the Cajón Negro hot springs, is distributed to the pools via wooden conduits under the walkway, where it's further heated to bring it to just the right temperature for bathing. Seventeen hot pools, spread out over nearly a quarter of a mile (half a kilometer) provide both sociable and secluded spots to bathe in the warm waters. Lined with slate, the pools shimmer aquamarine and ocher in the sunlight. The vivid red of the boardwalks was inspired by the colors used in local, traditional textiles. This is not intended as a luxury resort: everything has a natural, primitive aesthetic. Next to each pool there is a red, turf-roofed wooden hut with lockers and decks to relax on. Germàn del Sol specializes in designing innovative ways to relate to the Chilean landscape. The walkway makes jagged twists and turns through deciduous forest and past ferns clinging to cliff faces, as steam rises from the surrounding pools. It's designed to be a sylvan, otherworldly, and magical experience.

The State Historical Museum | **Vladimir Sherwood**
Moscow, Russia
1883

Located at No. 1 Red Square, Moscow's State Historical Museum was established in 1872 by Alexander II and was officially opened in 1883 to mark the coronation of Alexander III. With a collection of around 4.5 million objects, the museum receives a million visitors every year, half of whom are under eighteen. It presents a narrative of a thousand years of Russian history, as well as the history of northeastern Eurasian civilizations from the early Paleolithic Age to the present. The museum was designed by Vladimir Sherwood (whose surname came from his English engineer father). Sherwood won a competition that stipulated the new museum should reference specific Russian medieval buildings such as the wooden palace in Kolmenskoye and

churches in Vologda and Yaroslavl. The project was named "Fatherland" and the building's Russian Revival style, the Eastern equivalent of Neo-Gothic, features ornate cornices, turrets, terraces, and crenellations. The red, of course, is highly symbolic of the nation of Russia: the word for red, *krasnya*, is very close to the word for beautiful, *krasivy*; its Communist connotations came later. The brickwork facade is particularly complex—in 1876, 7,260 masons and several hundred builder's handymen were involved in creating it. The interior is equally impressive, with thirty-nine halls, each decorated by different artists. During the Stalinist era, the halls connected with the tsars were vandalized, and the museum remained closed for fifteen years.

"Red was the sunrise on the dawn of his creation."

| Carole King | Composer and Singer-Songwriter (1942–) |

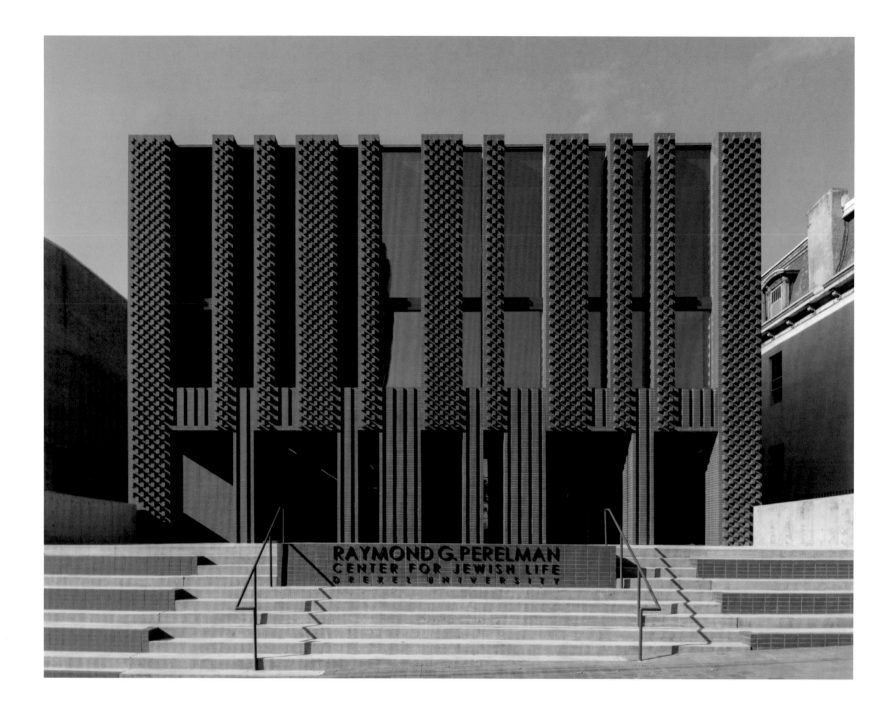

Center for Jewish Life at Drexel University | **Stanley Saitowitz/Natoma Architects**
Philadelphia, Pennsylvania, USA
2016

Drexel University is a private research institute in the University City area of Philadelphia. Hillel is the Foundation for Jewish Campus Life and is the largest student organization in the world, supporting Jewish students at more than 550 universities. Its base at Drexel, Hillel House—also named the Raymond G. Perelman Center for Jewish Life—is a place to meet, learn, study, and worship. Each of the building's four levels is devoted to different activities: community, learning, and prayer on the ground, first, and second floors, plus a support level in the basement with services such as kitchens, storage, and mechanical equipment. The most striking aspect is its front facade, designed in the form of an abstracted *menorah*, the branched

candle-holder used in Jewish homes and synagogues. The center is clad with locally sourced red brick of the kind used throughout the neighborhood. The brick is arranged in a textured pattern to evoke the *tallit*, the prayer shawls used in Jewish communities. Brick and glazing are arranged in strips of irregular width, also suggesting the stripes of a barcode, giving the center's design a contemporary twist. The top floor is reserved for Shabbat (sanctity): there is a library and worship areas devoted to three different strands of Judaism: conservative, orthodox, and reform groups. These are all clustered around a central, empty courtyard that emphasizes unity in the faith.

Brick Curtain House | **Design Work Group**
| **Surat, India**
| **2016**

This modern, spacious family home in the port city of Surat, in Gujurat, has an undulating brick facade that provides screening from the intense sun. The client was a local public figure who needed to meet with community members in the front part of the house, and wanted the rear reserved for family life. Located at the intersection of two roads, a decision was made to divide the house into two distinct zones, with the public and living areas in a projecting space at the front, facing west, and the private areas on the quieter, inner side, facing southwest. A bulging brick screen was built to create shading and ventilation in the hot, humid climate. Inspired by Indian *jali*—perforated or latticed stone screens—eighty-three rows of brick were used. The weight of the screen meant that the supporting wall had to be reinforced by five horizontal and seven vertical bars. Concave and convex bulges in the screen were placed at strategic points to create shading and cooling effects. Where the curtain reaches terraces on either side of the living room, gaps were left in the screen to allow views onto the street. The red-orange brick provides a warm aesthetic in the double-height living room, and contrasts with the gray concrete used widely throughout. Furniture inside the house is in complementary tones of brown and orange.

Micro Health Laboratory | **m3architecture/PHAB Architects**
Gatton, Queensland, Australia
2001

This project is a virtuoso exploration of brick's creative possibilities. m3architecture were commissioned to create a new Micro Health Laboratory as part of the University of Queensland. Strict regulations meant that the laboratory, a simple orthogonal box, had to be literally sealed from the outside world to prevent the escape of any contaminants. Those conditions were complied with to the letter in the design; the architects then set about envisioning an external "skin" for the laboratory using brick. They collaborated with PHAB and artist Ashley Paine to realize this next stage. Paine, who is also an architect (now running PHAB) and a senior lecturer at the Queensland School of Architecture, had completed a series of abstract self-portraits

between 2001 and 2002 made up of horizontal markings: these were the inspiration for the exterior pattern. Details from these works were abstracted and incorporated into three sides of the building's facade. Their ornate intricacy forms a dramatic contrast with the blank white of the building's interior lab spaces. The bricks were sculpted with a hammer and bolster (a chisel for slicing brick): two brick types and two cut types were used to create a pattern. In this way, the building shows the work of the human hand, giving it a tactile and anachronistic, aged appearance.

Dovecote Studio | **Haworth Tompkins**
Snape, England, UK
2009

Dovecote Studio is part of Snape Maltings, an arts campus in Suffolk created from derelict industrial buildings now converted into concert halls, art galleries, restaurants, and retail spaces. From composer Benjamin Britten's initial vision of building a music auditorium on the site, the complex has expanded since the late 1950s, hosting the annual international Aldeburgh Festival. Located on the River Alde with its serene reed beds and abundant birdlife, Snape Maltings is an evocative site, powerfully fusing the industrial and the natural. This jewel-like studio building has cleverly used the remnants of a Victorian dovecote (a building to house pigeons and doves) as its outer shell, inserting a Cor-Ten steel structure within the almost derelict ruin.

This was prefabricated and carefully craned into the crumbling shell. Inside, the studio is lined with bright, light plywood. The flexible space can be used by visual artists (northern light floods the studio through a skylight), for music rehearsals, as a place to write or as a meeting space. Minimal repairs were made to the ruin structure before the new shell was added, and vegetation around the brickwork was purposely left, to allow natural growth to run its course—a sign of both decay and regeneration. Under gray skies, the Cor-Ten steel is a muted rust-red, but in sunlight it is transfigured into a gorgeous, glowing, burnt orange.

Puck Building | **Albert and Herman Wagner**
New York City, New York State, USA
1886

In the heart of lower Manhattan, the Puck Building—designed by Albert and Herman Wagner and completed in the late nineteenth century—forms part of New York's high-rise, high-density urban fabric. Built of terracotta-colored red brick and rising to nine storeys, it's an example of Romanesque Revivalism—a style most easily identifiable by its use of rounded, symmetrical arches. Largely without ornament, except for that in brick, the architects adorned the building with two gilded figures of Puck, the mischievous character in Shakespeare's *A Midsummer Night's Dream*, designed by Henry Baerer. (One of the statues directs a mirror down the street, reflecting passersby on one of the city's busiest thoroughfares). Typical of its era, the building has a steel structure. In the Puck Building, this punctuates the facade with splashes of a soft, deep green—including an external staircase—creating a complementary contrast with the red of its mass. Despite its scale, its color allows it to stand apart from its neighbors. In this vibrant city, the building embodies the ambitions of the place it inhabits: bold, brash, self-assured.

Santa Monica Church | **Vicens + Ramos**
Rivas-Vacia Madrid, Spain
2016

This striking Cor-Ten steel creation is a bold and extraordinary re-imagination of traditional ecclesiastical architecture. Madrid-based architects Vicens + Ramos say that their main inspiration was conveying the passion of the priests for their church and congregation. Exuberant but also rational, its ingenious design of interlocking geometric forms and its bright orange-red color combine to create a startling landmark for the suburb of Rivas-Vaciamadrid. The church was built in response to the mushrooming population of the area. As well as the worship space, the complex contains offices and accommodation for two priests. The building's plan is based on the early Christian symbol of a fish. A pyramidal projection rises up at the church's east end to form its tail, and the opposite end resembles a gaping fish's mouth. The architects took a key element of church architecture—the spire—and converted it into multiple prismic forms with rectangular terminations. Both outside and inside, these projections are central in creating the building's emotional impact. At the presbytery end, they cluster and repeat, pointing in different directions. Far from being simply decorative, they house multiple rooflights, and inside the building they create sculptural forms. Javier Viver's Virgin and Santa Monica altar-wall statues are a figurative (and slightly surreal) contrast with the building's pure abstraction.

Institute of Functional Biology and Genomics | **Mata and Associates**
| **Salamanca, Spain**
| **2010**

The human genome and the way that cells grow are the main research interests of the Institute of Functional Biology and Genomics. It's a joint venture between the Consejo Superior de Investigaciones Científicas (CSIC) and the University of Salamanca. The building, on the university campus, consists of a simple four-storey rectangular block. Its vivid red makes it stand out against the other generic buildings in the area, with obvious connotations of blood and the human body. The topography of the site varies up to 20 feet (6 meters) in height from one end to another, and this was put to use as a way of creating different zones in the building—the lower end for car access, and the higher end for pedestrians. The compact plan is organized

around four vertical spaces within the building that bring light into its core. The facade is also interrupted by four recesses, allowing even more light in, wrapped in a semi-transparent glass screen with a pattern inspired by genetic-coding processes. At the north end there is an auditorium, which also houses the main entrance to the institute. The building's southern end cantilevers outward massively, supported by large concrete brackets. This marks the other entrance and provides a sheltered outdoor exhibition area. A generous, terraced landscaped space surrounds the block.

The Digit | **Anagram Architects**
New Delhi, India
2014

This office building was designed for one of the largest outdoor-media companies in India. As such, it was important that it would be uncompromising and attention-grabbing, just like one of their billboard advertisements. The architects were interested in the idea of identity—that of the company and the individuals working for it—as well as the importance of the clients' corporate vision to the whole enterprise. They chose "the most common imprint of identity, the thumbprint" as the key design idea. The 3,993-square-foot (371-square-meter) building was therefore designed in a semi-elliptical form, representing a thumb. This also gave the advantage of creating variety in the local built environment: the rest of the street consisted of an unbroken line of rectangular facades. As the floors ascend, the occupancy decreases and the seniority of staff increases, the uppermost being devoted to the director's office. The building's front is covered by a red screen perforated with disk-shaped openings, reducing heat from the sun and noise from the busy street below. Within the facade, a likeness of the company's logo has been created by reattaching the stamped-out disks and allowing them to move, via a pivot mechanism, so they flutter in the breeze. Continuing the theme inside, the lobby's ceiling is in the form of various ribbons of metal curved to form the shape and detail of a thumbprint.

10Cal Tower | **Supermachine Studio**
Bang Saen Beach, Thailand
2014

Positioned at the edge of a park close to Bang Saen Beach, Thailand, this pigmented concrete staircase offers a labyrinthine game of hide-and-seek. According to the designers, the arrangement of the structure began by questioning conventional play spaces, in which children are free, while their carers are left watching passively. Branching and complex, the installation is reminiscent of Escher's puzzling, imaginary, visual games; ascent and descent—two movements we often taken for granted—are subverted in a game of interlocking balconies, openings, and voids. In time, the installation will accommodate plants and creeping vines that will, by bringing contrast, heighten the tone of the concrete's pigment. The ocher-red of the concrete shell has another character at night. Illuminated from within, the structure glows—its brightness resonates with and reflects its deep-red surface—and becomes a beacon. At its top, the installation has spectacular views over the seafront and beach—a place to pause and reflect, as well as catch your breath (climbing at a normal pace from its bottom to its top consumes, we are told, ten calories!).

Fort Cortina | **Karelse & den Besten/TPAHG Architecten**
Amsterdam, The Netherlands
2011

This Amsterdam headquarters for a gift retailer, Cortina, was designed by a graphics agency. Cortina were one of the first clients of Karelse & den Besten, and had to find new premises. The graphic designers were originally asked to handle the signage for the new space, but eventually ended up planning an entire building, collaborating with a construction management firm, TPAHG Architecten. Karelse & den Besten were inspired by the clay-red, orthogonal forms and color of Moroccan forts. The slightly industrial, utilitarian forms they devised seemed to suit the location, the site of a former shipyard in the north of the city. The three storeys of offices and storage space are arranged around a courtyard, the inner walls of which are clad with cedar. The staggered floorplate allows for balconies and patios overlooking this space, and the building has a sedum roof garden. The most striking feature of the project is the brick used: the clay has been mixed with metal shavings to add glints of light and a contrasting color to the facade. In a playful touch, the doors to the loading bays have been punctured with circular openings—these cast lovely abstract patterns of light on what could otherwise be a drab, utilitarian space. A fourth-floor lookout tower creates a quirky, fortress-like profile. Whether the building's name is any reference to the 1970s car, the Ford Cortina, is unconfirmed, but it seems entirely possible.

The Ulma Family Museum | **Nizio Design International**
Markowa, Poland
2016

The village of Markowa is home to a museum commemorating the Ulma family, who gave shelter to eight Jews during the German occupation of Poland during World War II. Photographer Josef Ulma and his wife Wiktoria lived in the small settlement east of Kraków with their six children. It was probably 1942 when they took in eight Jews from the local area: Saul Goldmann and his four sons, and the two daughters and great-granddaughter of Chaim Goldman. The Ulmas' secret got out and on 24 March 1944, the German and Polish police arrived at their house. They shot the Jews first and then the Ulmas, including Wiktoria's unborn child, killing seventeen people in the space of a few minutes. The concrete-framed museum's architecture is inspired by the form of a primitive house, gabled at one end and tapering dramatically to a point—a poignant symbol of shelter and safety juxtaposed with forms implying anxiety and threat. The weathered, Cor-Ten steel shell suggests the passage of time. Inside, there is a glass structure representing a 1:1 reconstruction of the family home. At the point where the building tapers most is a narrow fissure, which lets a sliver of daylight in—a metaphor for hope in adversity.

Poplen Leisure and Youth Club | **Cornelius Vöge**
Jyllinge, Denmark
2012

This imaginative and sensitively designed youth center is in Jyllinge, a small town on the eastern shores of Roskilde Fjord with about 10,000 inhabitants. The project was a full refurbishment of an existing building and extension to its west, taking the total floor area to 6,458 square feet (600 square meters). The multipurpose center is located between a 1970s housing estate and an old village, so the decision was made to paint it bright red to create an identity of its own, using the color of local fishing huts as inspiration. The roof is the same color as the facades to create a clearly defined form and shape. The barn-like structure is also inspired by the local rural architecture, with its sharply pitched roof and lofty inner space. The building caters for all kinds of activities and personalities: as well as there being a large, indoor area for sports and games, there are five slightly cantilevering miniature rooms projecting from the building, which provide more intimate nooks for quieter conversations or for those who just want to read. Inside it's light and bright, clad with pale wood throughout. There is even a multifaceted climbing wall.

House for a Drummer | **Bornstein Lyckefors**
Karna, Sweden
2016

This house was built for a single father whose interests were drumming, sailing, and nature. He wanted a countryside home for weekends with his two children that could be a social, dynamic space, but also welcoming and intimate when he was alone. The house was built on the site of an old country store and warehouse that had burned down, and this backstory became a reference for the new house. Built entirely of wood, it was painted Swedish falu red. At 1,755 square feet (163 square meters) in area, the home's floors intertwine because of an open section cut through the house. This creates a sense of openness and visibility of the upper levels and allows light to permeate all spaces. The ground floor is made of a seamless concrete slab, while the other floors have varying heights and formats. Plywood is used for walls and shelving, and gives the home a simple, uncomplicated feel. The architects were inspired by Alfred Loos's ideas of *Raumplan*—ordering and sizing rooms in a home according to their function. Thus, there is a balance kept between open social spaces and cozier nooks for quiet reading—and, of course, there is a place for drumming.

"Everyone knows that yellow, orange, and red suggest ideas of joy and plenty. I can paint you the skin of Venus with mud, provided you let me surround it as I will."

Eugène Delacroix | **Artist (1798–1863)**

Index

Page numbers in italics refer to illustrations

Image Credits

Every reasonable effort has been made to acknowledge the ownership of copyright for photographs included in this volume. Any errors that may have occurred are inadvertent, and will be corrected in subsequent editions provided notification is sent in writing to the publisher.

Agaligo Studio: 39; Aitor Ortiz: 43; Alexey Naroditskiy, courtesy of Vitruvius and Songs: 20; Amédé Mulin: 160; Anagram Architects: 209; Anders Blomqvist / Getty Images: 107; Anders Blomqvist / Getty Images: 108; André Pihl/Wingårdhs: 123; Anthony Palmer / Alamy Stock Photo: 178; Arcaid Images / Alamy Stock Photo: 70; Archidev: 18; Archive Olgiati: 196; Bas Termeer: 59; © Beijing Hetuchuangyi Images Co,. Ltd . / Dreamstime.com: 102–103; Bornstein Lyckefors: 214–15; Brad Wheeler: 90–91; BFM Architekten: 66–67; Bryan Mullennix World View / Alamy Stock Photo: 26; Cheng Franco Arquitectos: 138–139; Christian Richters: 114, 165; Christian Vogt: 156; Claude thibault / Alamy Stock Photo: 21; Coaster / Alamy Stock Photo: 29; Collection Artedia/ VIEW: 199; ©Christian Richters: 134–135; Craig Ferguson /Getty Images: 116–117; Dan Glasser: 184; ©Daria Scagliola & Stijn Brakkee: 146; Design Work Group: 203; Diego Grandi / Alamy Stock Photo: 81; © Do Ho Suh, courtesy Lehmann Maupin Gallery, New York: 150; DnA: 177; Ernesta Caviola: 179; Ernesta Caviola, courtesy of Peluffo&Partners: 145; F A A B Architektura: 126–127; Far East Hospitality: 162; Fernando Guerra FG+SG: 163, 192; Fernando Alda: 143, 151; Filippo Simonetti: 133; GG-Loop: 144; Germán del Sol: 198; Gonçalo Byrne/ Fernando Guerra | FG+SG: 174; Guido Erbring: 72; Guy Charneau: 68; Haobo Wei / West-line Studio: 92; Hans Pattist/ NIO architecten: 75; Henning Larsen Architects: 105; Hufton + Crow: 36–7, 120–121; Hans Pattist/ NIO architecten: 93; Heinrich Helfenstein: 193; ©Hiroshi Ueda: 110, 194; imageBROKER / Alamy Stock Photo: 132; © imageBROKER/Alamy: 183; Inigo Bujedo Aguirre/VIEW: 166; Isabelle Cornet: 78; Iwan Baan: 149; Jakub Certowicz / courtesy of Cricoteka: 148, 197; Jaime Navarro , courtesy of Rojkind Arquitectos: 76; James Morris/VIEW: 191; João Morgado / Future Architecture Thinking: 16–17; John Winder: 95; Jose Javier Gallardo: 19; José María Díez Laplaza, amas4arquitectura: 140; Julien Lanoo, courtesy of NEXT architects: 172–3; Kongjian Yu, Turenscape: 80; Kris Van den Bosch/ Close to Bone: 189; KUSHNER COMPANIES: 206; © Lawrence Anderson, Courtesy LOHA: 111; Leonardo Finotti: 94; Linkins, Jon. Courtesy m3architecture: 204; Loop Images / Getty Images: 54–5; Luis Ferreira Alves: 158–159; Margutti Associati / Arkispazio: 24; Martin King: 50; MATHEISL / Contributor: 44–45, 190; Martin Ruegner/Getty Images: 128; Masato Kawano / 3Gatti: 74; Matthew Placek: 69; Mata y Asociados: 208; © Maurice Savage/Alamy: 164; Michelle Nastasi/VIEW: 56; MJ Photography / Alamy Stock Photo: 52; Mieneke Andeweg-van Rijn/Alamy: 87; Nam-Sun Lee / Archiworkshop: 157; Niels Nygaard, Arkitema Architects: 27; Nico Saieh, courtesy of Gonzalo Mardones Viviani: 115; Nigel Young, courtesy of Foster and Partners: 180–1; Nils Petter Dale: 73; Nizio Design International / Lech Kwartowicz: 212; © Ossip van Duivenbode: 38; NRJA: 57; Pablo Enriquez, courtesy of Katharina Grosse: 77; Paul Rivera: 34–5; Paul Warchol: 25; © Paúl Rivera, courtesy of Roger Ferris + Partners: 71; Penique Productions: 60; Philip Vile: 22; PETER LUNDSTRÖM: 86; Philippe Ruaul: 125; Philippe Rault: 53; Philippe Ruault: 112–3; Pratan Ounpitipong/ Getty Images: 176; Raphael GAILLARDE /Getty Images: 98–99; Raymond Boyd/Getty Images: 131; Ricardo Santonja: 147; Ricardo Bofill: 195; Richard Pare: 41; Richard Sowersby / Alamy Stock Photo: 168–9 ; Richard Barnes, Stanley Saitowitz | Natoma Architects: 202; Rob 't Hart: 88; Roberto Michel / Alamy Stock Photo: 161; Robin Hayes: 104; © Roland Halbe: 23; Sander Meisner: 188; Santo Eduardo Di Miceli, courtesy of Cerejeira Fontes Arquitectos: 79; Scott E Barbour/Getty Images: 185; Simon Kennedy , courtesy of Aberrant Architecture: 106; Shigeo Ogawa: 124; Søren Harder Nielsen, courtesy of Cornelius + Voge: 213; Steve Massam: 62–3; Stufish Entertainment Architects:129; Supermachine Studio: 210; ©Takuji Shimmura, Jean-Paul Viguier et Associés, Architecture et Urbanism: 89; Tate Images: 96; Theo Peekstok, courtesy of Groosman: 28; Tomasz Kurek, Studio Architektoniczne Kwadrat: 182; The Condensery: 61, 130; Timothy Hursley/ Marlon Blackwell: 46–7; Tord-Rickard Söderström: 84–5; Vanessa Rudloff for Shevaun Williams: 30–31; Vector Architects: 175; Vegar Moen: 58; Verwoerdt, Dirk: 167; Vicens + Ramos: 207; View Pictures / Getty Images: 205; View Pictures/UIG via Getty Images: 122; Wison Tungthunya: 42; Werner Huthmacher: 141; Yael Pincus, courtesy of Jacob Peres: 109; Yayoi Kusama inc.: 97; Yuri Palmin, courtesy of Totan Kuzembaev: 40; Yves Gellie: 154–155

Quotations

Albers, Josef (1888–1976), American-German artist
– Page 119. *Interaction of Color*, published by Yale University Press in 1963.

Anonymous
– page 9. *Trattato dell'Arte della Seta* (Treaty of Silk Art), c1300

Blass, Bill (1922–2002), American fashion designer
– Page 49. Source unknown.

Burns, Robert (1759–1796), Scottish poet
– Page 9. *A Selection of Scots Songs, Harmonized, improved with Simple and Adapted Graces*, published in 1794.

Delacroix, Eugene (1798–1863), French artist
– Page 217. Source Unknown.

Haring, Keith (1958–1990), American artist
– Page 65. Interview with Sylvie Couderc, Bordeaux on December 16, 1985.

Jarman, Derek (1942–1994), British film director, artist, and author
– Page 31. *Chroma: A Book of Colour*, published by Century in 1994.

Killing Joke (1978–), British rock band
– Page 101. Turn to Red written by Jaz Coleman, Kevin "Geordie" Walker, Martin "Youth" Glover, Paul Ferguson, © Malicious Damage, EP released in 1979.

King, Carole (1942–), American composer and singer-songwriter
– Page 201. "Seeing Red," written by Carole King, © Capitol, released as part of the album *Touch The Sky* in 1979.

Lissitzky, El (1890–1941), Russian artist and polemicist
– Page 11. Poster illustrated in 1919.

Louboutin, Christian (Born 1964), French fashion designer
– Page 153. *The Colour Code*, Klara Goldy on Lulu.com in 2014.

Matisse, Henri (1869–1954), French painter
– Page 83. *Synesthesia and the Arts* by Dani Cavallaro, published by MacFarland, in 2013.

Motherwell, Robert (1915–1991), American painter and print maker
– Pages 11 and 171. *The Writings of Robert Motherwell*, published by California University Press in 2007.

Picasso, Pablo (1881–1973), Spanish artist
– Page 33. *The Yale Book of Quotations*, edited by Fred Shapiro, published by Yale University Press in 2006.

Pamuk, Orhan (1952–), Turkish novelist and recipient of the 2006 Nobel Prize in Literature
– Page 7. *My Name is Red*, published by Faber and Faber in 2011.

Pliny the Elder (Gaius Plinius Secundus) (23–79 AD), Roman writer and natural philosopher
– Page 7. *Natural History*, first published c77–79.

Titian (1488–1576), Italian painter
– Page 187. View attributed to Titian by the Venetian artist and art dealer Marco Boschini (1613–78); *Titian: His Life* by Sheila Hale published by HarperPress in 2012.

Vreeland, Diana (1903–1989), French fashion editor
– Page 137. *DV* by Diana Vreeland, published by Alfred A. Knopf in 1984.

Williams, Carlos William (1883–1963), American poet
– Page 11. "Classic Scene" in *Selected Poems*, published by Penguin Modern Classics in 2000.